Berlitz

REYKJAVÍK
POCKET GUIDE

Walking Eye
mobile app

Discover the world's best destinations with the Insight Guides Walking Eye app, available to download for free in the App Store and Google Play.

The container app provides easy access to fantastic free content on events and activities taking place in your current location or chosen destination, with the possibility of booking, as well as the regularly-updated Insight Guides travel blog: Inspire Me. In addition, you can purchase curated, premium destination guides through the app, which feature local highlights, hotel, bar, restaurant and shopping listings, an A to Z of practical information and more. Or purchase and download Insight Guides eBooks straight to your device.

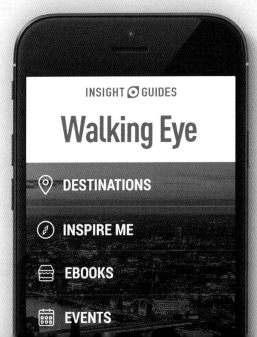

TOP 10 ATTRACTIONS

HALLGRÍMSKIRKJA
The tower of this striking church enjoys stunning city views. See page 28.

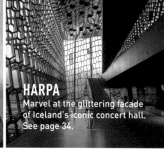

HARPA
Marvel at the glittering facade of Iceland's iconic concert hall. See page 34.

NATIONAL MUSEUM OF ICELAND
Investigate Iceland's Viking past at the excellent National Museum. See page 42.

THE OLD HARBOUR
Take to the waves on a whale-watching trip. See page 45.

REYKJAVÍK ART MUSEUM

Iceland's most famous artists are on display at Hafnarhús, Kjarvalsstaðir and Ásmundarsafn art galleries. See pages 44, 52 and 54.

REYKJAVÍK MARITIME MUSEUM

Shudder at shipwrecks and the harshness of life at sea. See page 48.

PERLAN

The high-tech science museum and planetarium showcases the power of volcanoes, earthquakes and glaciers. See page 57.

ÁRBÆJARSAFN OPEN-AIR MUSEUM

Time-travel to 19th-century Iceland at this village of historical houses. See page 55.

BLUE LAGOON

Bathe at this world-famous spa, set surreally in a vast black lava field. See page 67.

GOLDEN CIRCLE

Visit waterfalls, hot springs and Þingvellir National Park on the must-do Golden Circle tour. See page 65.

A PERFECT DAY

9.00am

Breakfast

Sip a wake-up espresso at one of Reykjavík's many cosy cafés, or go full Icelandic at Café Loki (Lokastígur 28) and start the day with homemade flatbread, sheep's-head jelly, turnips and cottage cheese.

10.00am

Shoreline stroll

Head to Harpa for stunning city, sea and harbour views. A short walk east leads to the iconic *Sólfar* sculpture. To the west, check out Icelandic pop art at the Hafnarhús gallery, explore the city's maritime museum or retrace the voyages of the Viking settlers at the bloodthirsty Saga Museum.

12.00pm

Lunch at the harbour

Stop for a bowl of fish soup and fresh-baked bread at Reykjavík's oldest restaurant, Kaffivagninn, at Grandagarður 10.

2.00pm

Traditional Reykjavík

Catch bus 14 to City Hall, and admire the abundant birdlife on Tjörnin pond. Take a walk through Austurvöllur Square, the city's traditional heart, where you'll find the Icelandic Parliament and Reykjavík's modest cathedral, Dómkirkjan. Stop at the excellent Settlement Exhibition on Aðalstræti to see saga manuscripts and an original Viking farmhouse.

3.30pm

Retail therapy

Shop for souvenirs in the quirky boutiques along Reykjavík's main street, Laugavegur. Source Blue Lagoon skincare products (No. 15), Icelandic music (Smekkleysa, No. 28) and cutting-edge fashion (Kronkron, No. 63b), or branch off up Skólavörðustígur for Icelandic sweaters (The Handknitting Association of Iceland, No. 19).

IN REYKJAVÍK

7.00pm

Fine dining

There are many excellent restaurants in the city centre. Two options for cosy dining are the charmingly rustic Messinn (Lækjargata) and hip hangout Snaps Bistro Bar (Óðinstorg).

9.00pm

Relax or rev up

Icelanders start partying late. This is the time to catch 40 winks at your hotel in preparation for a long night; or if you're keen to commence, Gaukurinn (Tryggvagata 22) has karaoke, stand-up comedy, open-mic nights or gigs starting between 8pm and 10pm every night.

5.00pm

Steam and soak

Reykjavík's seven soothing geothermal pools are restorative. The most central is Sundhöllin, on Barónsstígur. It has indoor and outdoor pools, hot pots to relax and gossip in and a view of Hallgrímskirkja from the sun deck.

12.00am

On the town

The city centre is packed with lively bars and clubs. Start with a well-made cocktail at dressy Apótek (Austurstræti 16). Kaffibarinn (Bergstaðastræti 1) is a long-standing classic that never loses its cool. Connoisseurs will love Microbar (Vesturgata 2), which serves an interesting array of craft beers. Húrra (Tryggvagata 22) is a great all-rounder for gigs, music and dancing. Grab a hotdog (*pylsur*) with mustard from an all-night food stand on the way back to your hotel.

CONTENTS

🎯 FEATURES

INTRODUCTION

Reykjavík, the world's most northerly capital, is a compact, cosmopolitan city, its narrow streets filled with small, brightly painted buildings and wild white arctic light. Several show-stopping landmarks – the rocket-like church of Hallgrímskirkja, the glittering Harpa concert hall – are a testament to this tiny city's can-do attitude and ambition. Over a third of the country's population lives in the capital, where they enjoy a rich cultural life, fresh air and a magnificent location.

The steely grey waters of the North Atlantic surround the city, surging into countless bays and inlets, and bringing whales, dolphins, seals and abundant birdlife to Reykjavík's shores. Standing by the water's edge, you can look out towards majestic snow-capped mountains, Snæfellsjökull glacier and brooding volcanoes and lavafields to the east, just a day-trip away.

However, should you choose to stay in the city, you'll be rewarded with an extensive bar and restaurant scene and some buzzing nightlife, too. Reykjavík also boasts an impressive array of museum and galleries, regularly changing art exhibitions and a packed calendar of festivals and events, particularly in the giddy months of summer. The city's energetic and distinctive cultural scene is a constant source of fascination, yet Reykjavík retains a certain slow pace and almost rustic charm that makes it unique among the world's capitals.

Iceland works almost exclusively in English, so a lack of Icelandic is not usually a problem. Everything you will want to see in Reykjavík is either within walking distance or a short bicycle, bus or taxi ride away. Facilities are constantly improving, and the last 10 years have seen a boom in tour and activity companies: the adventurous can book a tempting array of horseriding, hiking, caving, diving and whale-watching trips with city operators.

UNDERGROUND DRAMA

In geological terms, Iceland is a mere babe, composed of some of the youngest rocks on earth and still being formed. Over the centuries, eruptions have spewed vast fields of lava across the island's surface and projected choking clouds of ash high into the air, blocking out the sunlight, blighting crops and killing thousands. A tiny taster of Iceland's volcanic power was seen in 2010, when the Eyjafjallajökull eruptions brought European air travel to a halt for six days, costing the airline industry an estimated £1.1 billion (€1.3 billion). Every day there are thousands of minor earthquakes, although most are only detectable by seismologists.

The presence of so much natural energy just below ground makes it possible not just to see the awesome power of nature, but to feel, hear and smell it. The limitless reserves of geothermal energy that have produced such a varied terrain also supply heat and power to Iceland's homes, and the 'rotten egg' smell of sulphur is unmistakable whenever you turn on a tap or hop in the shower. Dams across fast-flowing glacial rivers provide the nation with

Eyjafjallajökull eruption

Exploring Reykjavík on two wheels

more than enough hydroe-
lectrically generated power
to meet its needs.

As well as heating
homes and offices, all
this hot water is used to
create swimming pools
across the island. These
are a vital part of Icelandic
social life, with people
gathering in the hot tubs
and steam rooms to catch
up on the local gossip.

POLLUTION-FREE LAND

For Reykjavíkers, keeping
their city clean and pollution-free is a top priority. It's with jus-
tifiable pride that they boast that the water from countryside
streams and rivers is drinkable, due in no small part to the
general lack of heavy industry. The air in Reykjavík is bitingly
fresh and among the cleanest you'll find anywhere in Europe. In
a few parts of the country, Iceland's pristine landscape has been
marred by dams built to power enormous aluminium smelting
plants, projects that have roused huge controversy. However, for
the main part, the environment is refreshingly unspoiled.

HIGH STANDARD OF LIVING

Reykjavík enjoys one of the highest standards of living of any city
in the world. A European nation, Iceland remains outside the
European Union mainly to protect its economically vital fishing
grounds. It has strong social institutions and a well-funded welfare
system. Few Icelanders are conspicuously rich, but there's little

urban poverty, and health care and education facilities throughout the country are highly developed. Reykjavík remains, though, the richest and most-sought after place to live in the country.

SMALL BUT PERFECTLY FORMED

In European terms, Reykjavík is a small and compact place – its population is around 123,000. Although Iceland is equal in size to England and has plenty of undeveloped land, roughly three out of every five Icelanders live in and around the capital. The population may be small, but it's clear from the cafés, restaurants and bars that this is a place where people know how to have a good time. However, the scene starts late, and the often eye-watering prices for alcohol and a decent meal force many locals to get their eating and a fair bit of their drinking done at home before they venture out.

GETTING OUT AND ABOUT

Since the late 1970s Iceland's only major road, a vast circular route around the coast, has linked village to town, countryside to capital. Most communities are found on or near the ring road, a short distance from the sea, where the land is at its flattest and most fertile. This narrow coastal plain, the only truly habitable part of the country, makes up just one-fifth of Iceland's total area.

Fortunately, much of the most impressive scenery is easily accessible from Reykjavík. The worthwhile Golden Circle tour from Reykjavík takes in the original Geysir, which gave its name to all geysers around the world; Gullfoss waterfall; and Þingvellir, the site of the Vikings' parliament and birthplace of the nation. Also a hit with visitors is the Blue Lagoon, an outdoor spa set in a dramatic lava wasteland. Day trips are also possible to the Snæfellsnes peninsula and

Celebrity culture

Keep your eyes peeled and there's a good chance you'll bump into someone famous in Reykjavík. Television personalities, popstars and politicians regularly stroll up and down the main street, Laugavegur, unhindered by body guards thanks to the open and unthreatening nature of Reykjavík society.

to the sparsely populated south coast, lined with glaciers and waterfalls. The Vestmannaeyjar, a short plane ride from the capital, give a taste of island life.

LONG DAYS OF SUMMER

The weather in Reykjavík is extremely changeable. Winters are cold and dark, with a moderate amount of snowfall. Light relief is provided at night by the spectral glow of the northern lights (*aurora borealis*). It's only in summer, when the temperatures rise and the long days are often bright and sunny, that Reykjavík can really be seen in its true colours – flowers are in full bloom, the air is alive with birdsong and the long summer nights barely show any sign of darkness. Remember that Reykjavík is at its most lively and animated between May and September – definitely the best time to visit. Similarly, the bus companies don't run a full service until late June, something to bear in mind if you're planning bus trips outside the capital. Domestic air schedules are similar in winter and summer, although flights can be disrupted by bad weather.

Despite the rigours of its landscape, Reykjavík – and indeed the rest of Iceland – is a very welcoming place. Its people aren't given to great outward shows of emotion, but they are intensely proud of their city and will offer an embrace that is as sincere as it is warm to the visitor who's willing to respect their capital's unique location on the very edge of the Arctic.

A BRIEF HISTORY

While elsewhere in Europe, civilisations, empires and dynasties came and went, Iceland remained uninhabited and undiscovered. It wasn't until the 8th century ad that Irish monks became the first people known to have set foot on the island, relishing its solitude. They left no physical trace behind either, nor, being all men, any new generations. Within 100 years the peace they had enjoyed was no longer: the Vikings were coming. Much of Iceland's Viking history was chronicled within a few hundred years of the first settlers setting foot on its shores. The *Landnámabók* (Book of Settlements) and *Íslendingabók* (Book of Icelanders), written in the 12th century, describe in detail the first permanent inhabitants. The sagas, dramatic tales of early Iceland penned 100 years later, give a lot more colour to the story in the form of fiction.

THE FOUNDING OF REYKJAVÍK

The country's first permanent settlers were Norwegians escaping political persecution and economic hardship at home. They found Iceland by accident, having already colonised parts of both

Landnámabók

Scotland and the Faroe Islands. The official 'First Settler' was Ingólfur Arnarson, who enjoyed his first winter so much that he went to fetch his extended family and friends to come and join him. They brought with them farm animals, paganism and Irish slaves, some of whom would cause mutiny and kill their owners. However, there was no indigenous population for the colonisers to evict or butcher, and the biggest threat they faced was from the elements. Having spent three years roaming Iceland's southern coast, Ingólfur eventually settled in 874 in

⊙ THE SAGAS

Between the 12th and 15th centuries, some of the great stories the Icelanders had previously passed on from generation to generation were written down. Collectively known as *The Sagas* (literally 'things told'), they are some of the most dramatic and compelling tales in world literature. Scholars argue about how historically accurate they are, but for good old-fashioned story telling they are unbeatable. They encompass kings' lives, stories of saints, poets and outlaws, and – most famously – the family sagas, detailing tragic feuds, fights and friendships over the generations. They are written in an unemotional style that makes the brutal fates of many of their characters even more shocking. The manuscripts were collected for posterity by Árni Magnússon (1663–1730) and taken off to Copenhagen for safety, but most were then lost in a terrible fire. Árni himself braved the flames to rescue some of them. The surviving sagas weren't returned to Iceland until long after Independence. Perhaps wary of their troubled history, the authorities in Reykjavík keep them under lock and key, although some are put on display at the Culture House.

the bay that is now home to Reykjavík. It was here that his high seat pillars – a potent symbol of Viking chieftainship – were finally washed up after being tossed overboard from Ingólfur's boat when he first approached Icelandic shores three or four years earlier. He named the location *reykjavík* ('smoky bay') after the plumes of steam he saw issuing from nearby hot springs.

Statue of Ingólfur Arnarson

These first Icelanders established farms in the rather more hospitable parts of the country. Some basic laws were already in place: a man could claim as much land as he could light bonfires around in one day, so long as each one could be seen from the previous fireplace. Women could have as much land as a heifer could walk around in a day. Inevitably disputes broke out, which the local chieftains had to resolve. When they failed, there could be bloody battles. Population growth was slow due to the severe climatic conditions and constant disease; indeed by 1786, the population of Reykjavík town barely numbered 176 souls.

THE FIRST PARLIAMENT

In ad 930 the chieftains got together and agreed on a relatively democratic system of government. A Commonwealth was established, with a national assembly or Alþingi meeting for two weeks every summer at Þingvellir, a flat plain southeast

What's in a name?

Although many Icelanders can trace their families back to the early settlers, family names do not exist. Instead, children absorb their father's first name into their own. A man named Eiríkur Gúðbrands-son might, for example, have a son named Leifur Eiríksson and a daughter named Þórdís Eiríksdóttir.

of Reykjavík which could be reached relatively easily from all parts of the country. Here, new laws would be agreed and infringements of old laws settled by a system of regional courts. The worst punishment was to be declared an outlaw and banished from the country.

The system wasn't perfect, and there were still some bloody battles – these were, after all, the descendants of Vikings, who valued courage and honour above all else. Nonetheless this period is now considered to have been a Golden Age, the Saga Age, full of great heroes and wise men.

FROM PAGANS TO CHRISTIANS

Soon, however, things were to change dramatically. Christianity had spread to northern Europe, and the zealous, if bloodthirsty, King Ólafur Tryggvason of Norway wanted Iceland for the new religion too. When his missionaries encountered resistance in the late 10th century, he was all for butchering the entire population until the Icelandic chieftain Gizur the White promised to have another go by more peaceful means. Fortunately the law speaker, who presided over the Alþingi, was at that time a widely respected figure. He persuaded both sides to agree to accept his decision in advance and then went off to meditate. He came back and announced that Iceland would become Christian, although pagans could continue to practise their beliefs in private.

Bishoprics, monasteries and schools quickly followed, and books were soon being written for the first time. As a sign of their independence the writers chose to do their work in Icelandic, not Latin. There were so few foreign influences in the centuries to come that the language they used is almost identical to the Icelandic spoken today.

All was not well in the land, however, and Iceland was about to enter its Dark Age. The Hekla volcano southeast of Reykjavík erupted in 1104, burying nearby farms; over-grazing and soil erosion from excessive tree-felling further reduced the amount of viable land. At the same time the church became greedy and, by imposing tithes, it split the formerly egalitarian society. Some chiefs, who were given church lands or made into senior clergy, found themselves increasingly rich and powerful. Before long the most important families started fighting for supremacy. The Alþingi, which had relied on people voluntarily accepting its authority, was now powerless to impose the law.

CIVIL WAR AND BLACK DEATH

Soon the country was in a state of civil war, which was ended only when Norway took sovereignty to help maintain order in 1262. Iceland kept many of its old laws, but 700 years of foreign domination had begun.

Tableau at the Saga Museum

◎ WHALES AND WHALING

For many visitors, Iceland's attitude to whaling is perplexing. The country has a very good record for environmental protection and an apparent deep respect for nature. Nevertheless, it continues to hunt endangered whale species.

Historically, the abundance of whales off Iceland's coasts meant whales were an important source of meat and oil, with even their bones being used for building materials, from early medieval times onwards. Commercial whaling began in earnest in 1948, when the Icelandic whaling company, Hvalur, was established. Hunting continued until 1989, when strong international pressure led to a pause. In 2003, Iceland announced its intention to begin 'scientific' whaling; and in 2006 it once again resumed the commercial hunt. Difficulties in exporting the whale meat to the Japanese market led to Hvalur cancelling hunting in 2016; but it resumed with a quota of 161 endangered fin whales in the 2018/2019 season.

Whaling once roused strong nationalistic feelings in Iceland, although passionate support for whaling has been dwindling. A 2018 poll indicates 34 percent of Icelanders are still in favour of commercial hunting, 34 percent against, and 31 percent have no opinion. Only around three percent of Icelanders eat whale regularly: tourists are now its main consumers within the domestic market, while the rest of the catch is exported to Japan when possible, for human consumption and for luxury dog treats.

The International Fund for Animal Welfare (IFAW) and Icelandic whale-watching operators (http://icewhale.is) run the 'Meet Us, Don't Eat Us' campaign to draw visitors' attention to the issue.

Revolts and skirmishes continued, while nature also took its toll. Harsh winters destroyed farm animals and crops, yet more eruptions covered parts of the country in ash and the Black Death arrived in Iceland, laying waste to half the population.

Those Icelanders still living were too busy struggling to survive to notice that Denmark had taken over the Norwegian

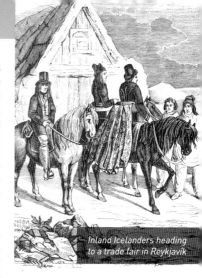

Inland Icelanders heading to a trade fair in Reykjavik

throne and was therefore their new master. But the Danes took little interest in their new acquisition, despite it possessing something the rest of Europe suddenly wanted: cod. Fishing brought new wealth to coastal landowners, but it brought new trouble, too.

English and German adventurers started appearing offshore, fighting among themselves, indulging in piracy and trying to control the trade in dried cod. The English got the upper hand, and this became known as the English Century. The Danes eventually realised that they were losing out financially. When Denmark tried to ban the English from the country, the latter killed the governor and started bringing in their canons. By 1532, however, the tide had turned, and the English leader was killed in renewed fighting with Germany. From then on England let the Danes and Germans fight among themselves and turned its attention elsewhere.

Jónas Hallgrímsson shown on the 10,000 króna bank note

THE REFORMATION

The Church was still a dominant force in the early 16th century, and when Scandinavia turned Lutheran in the 1530s it was inevitable that Iceland would soon follow suit. By the middle of the century the Protestant Reformation had been well and truly imposed on an unwilling population.

By this time, Denmark was gaining increased political authority over Iceland, and eventually complete control of the country was passed to Copenhagen. From 1602 all of Iceland's trade had to pass by law through a small group of Danish companies, a move that effectively bankrupted the country. Smallpox then wiped out almost a third of the impoverished population, and, just when it seemed as if matters could not get any worse, thousands more citizens were killed in 1783–4 by massive volcanic eruptions that poisoned almost the entire country and caused widespread famine. Denmark considered evacuating the whole surviving population, but decided instead to relax the trading laws a little and give the country a chance to recover.

As it did so, educated Icelanders looked to continental Europe and saw democracy stirring in once-powerful monarchies. Jónas Hallgrímsson, a poet, and Jón Sigurðsson, a historian, started a fledgling independence movement. By 1843 they succeeded in getting the Alþingi, suspended since 1800, revived as a consultative assembly. A decade later trade was freed up completely. Slowly, prosperity started to return.

In 1874 Denmark, now a constitutional monarchy, returned full legislative powers to the Alþingi. The tithe system was abolished, schooling became compulsory and the fishing industry was allowed to grow and prosper. By 1900 Iceland had its own political parties. In 1904 it was granted Home Rule and in 1918 gained independence in return for keeping the Danish king as monarch.

WAR AND PEACE

Iceland, now trading with both England and Germany, stayed neutral in World War I, although its growing economy was hit by the Great Depression of the 1930s. During World War II control of the North Atlantic was a key strategic objective, and first Britain, then the United States, landed forces in Iceland and occupied Reykjavík. Denmark was invaded and occupied by Germany, leaving Iceland to stand on its own two feet, finally declaring full independence on 17 June 1944. Reykjavík now became the capital of a sovereign country and inherited all the trappings of state including a president, fully fledged parliament and a seat at the United Nations.

Reykjavík's strategic location made the new government nervous as the Cold War gripped the western world. In response it joined the UN and then NATO, a controversial decision that provoked riots in Reykjavík which saw the parliament attacked and protestors tear-gassed – a rare outbreak of violence in Iceland.

When Iceland next went to war, however, it was with a fellow NATO country, Britain.

Jón Sigurðsson

Jón Sigurðsson (1811–1869) is remembered for his role in campaigning for independence from Denmark. Jón's birthday – 17 June – is now celebrated as Icelandic National Day.

Fortunately nobody was killed, and the so-called Cod Wars, that came and went for 30 years after 1952, were no more than a bit of naval muscle flexing. Britain objected to successive extensions to Iceland's territorial waters and sent patrol boats to protect its trawlers. In 1975 it ordered its frigates to ram Icelandic coast-guard ships, which had been cutting the cables of British trawlers. Eventually, in 1985, Reykjavík got its way, and 325km (200-mile) limits became the norm worldwide.

Although the European Union's stringent fisheries policy has deterred Reykjavík from joining that group, since the last quarter of the 20th century the country has been increasingly outward looking, attracting foreign businesses and visitors. In 1986 the world's media descended on Reykjavík for a nuclear summit between presidents Reagan and Gorbachev, which was famously held at Höfði House and raised the country's profile worldwide.

In 2008, the global financial crisis hit Iceland hard, with all three of Iceland's major banks failing, unemployment soaring to over nine percent and the government resigning in the face of angry protests. Austerity measures, emergency financial aid from the International Monetary Fund (IMF) and a huge growth in tourism all helped pull the country through its economic meltdown – by 2015, Iceland's GDP was at its former pre-crash levels. However the political fallout rumbles on to the present day, with prime ministers and governments being replaced in quick succession over issues such as whether Iceland should pay UK and Netherlands savers compensation for the collapse of its Icesave bank; austerity measures; EU membership; and financial irregularities revealed by the Panama Papers. In 2017, snap elections voted in the Left-Green prime minister Katrín Jakobsdóttir, leading a coalition government composed of parties from both the left and right.

Reykjavík is a forward-thinking capital city, happy to cooperate with the world community, yet reluctant to be dictated by it.

HISTORICAL LANDMARKS

874 Reykjavík is founded by Ingólfur Arnarson and his family.

930 Creation of the Alþingi parliament southeast of Reykjavík.

1000 Christianity is adopted as Iceland's official religion.

13th and 14th centuries Feuding between Norway and Denmark over the ruling of Iceland. Reykjavík loses power to Copenhagen.

1389 Huge eruption of Mt Hekla devastates farming land around Reykjavík. Black Death decimates the town.

1662–1854 Reykjavík traders hit by Danish trade monopoly.

1783 Laki volcano eruption poisons the land, causing famine in Reykjavík.

1800 Danish King abolishes the Alþingi; it is reinstated in 1843.

1904 Iceland is granted limited home rule and Reykjavík becomes the capital.

1918 Iceland made a sovereign state under the Act of Union with Denmark. Danish king is head of state.

1940 British forces arrive in Reykjavík to occupy Iceland.

1944 Independence from Denmark declared on 17 June.

1947 Last American soldiers leave Keflavík air base.

1948 US Marshall aid pours in to Iceland.

1949 Iceland becomes a founding member of NATO, provoking riots in Reykjavík. Police retaliate with tear gas.

1951 Keflavík air base re-established; 5,000 American troops arrive.

1952–76 Cod Wars (1952, 1958, 1972, 1975) with the UK.

1963 Surtsey island created by an underwater volcanic eruption.

1973 Volcanic eruption on Heimaey island.

1986 Reykjavík summit between presidents Reagan and Gorbachev.

1994 Iceland enters the European Economic Area.

2006 Commercial whaling resumes after a 17-year hiatus.

2008 Iceland's banks fail during the global financial crisis; angry protests in Reykjavík bring down the government.

2009 Iceland elects Jóhanna Sigurðardóttir, the world's first openly gay prime minister.

2010 Eyjafjallajökull eruptions bring chaos to European air traffic.

2018 The wettest summer since 1914 causes Iceland's largest landslide.

View of low-rise Reykjavík from
the cathedral

WHERE TO GO

Reykjavík, the world's northernmost capital, is a bright, colourful, friendly city. It may not be the world's largest, but it contains a surprising number of sights and activities. A huge amount of time, money and effort has gone into bringing its museums and galleries, public buildings, parks, sports facilities and cutting-edge restaurants up to international standards. You will very quickly get the sense that Icelanders are immensely proud of their country, and of Reykjavík in particular. They love living here, and want you to enjoy the delights that the city has to offer.

It doesn't take long to spot what makes Reykjavík so different. It's refreshingly small and green, with the laidback pace of a mid-sized town rather than the hyperactive hustle of a hard-nosed city. Although over a third of Icelanders live here, Reykjavík retains a friendly, almost rustic feel. Major roads wrap around its edges, but in the centre the streets are narrow and thronged with pedestrians. Everyone knows everyone, and traffic on the main shopping street Laugavegur often comes to a standstill when a driver stops to chat to a friend they've spotted. Cafés, bars, live music, art galleries, little museums and interesting one-off boutiques thrive. The sea is ever-present, with stunning glacier and mountain views across the water, and whales swimming in Faxaflói kirk. Reykjavík is a joy, not just for what it has but also for what it doesn't have: traffic jams, pollution, bleak high-rise buildings, high crime rates, tired, tight-lipped commuters hustling through packed streets... After just a short while you come to realise that Reykjavík has the best of a city with few of the drawbacks that can make other capitals such hard work.

Visitors to Reykjavík vary from those on city breaks and stopovers en route to North America, to others who are here

Finding true north

If Reykjavík feels a long way from anywhere, it's because it really is at the edge of the world. Situated at 64.08°N, it is the world's most northerly capital city. And at 21.55°W, it is Europe's most westerly.

for a longer exploration of Iceland. For those on a short visit, it's possible to see most of the city's main sights in a full day or two. The magnificent Hallgrímskirkja church is a must-see, as is Harpa concert hall with its glittering facade. Viking and saga fans are spoiled with the fabulous National Museum; the Culture House, where a beautiful 14th-century medieval manuscript is displayed; and the Settlement Exhibition, built around the remains of an excavated Viking Age farmhouse. Nature lovers can go bird-watching, or hop on a boat to spot minke whales, white-beaked dolphins and harbour porpoises. Leave another few days to explore some of the attractions a short journey from the capital – the Golden Circle, the Blue Lagoon or the waterfalls and glaciers of the south coast, for example.

The tourist industry works almost exclusively in English, and getting around is very easy. In Reykjavík the public transport system is clean and reliable, and many of the central sights can be explored comfortably on foot.

HALLGRÍMSKIRKJA AND AROUND

HALLGRÍMSKIRKJA

Massive **Hallgrímskirkja** ❶ (www.hallgrimskirkja.is; daily May–Sept 9am–9pm, Oct–Apr 9am–5pm; free, but charge for tower) sits like a rocket on a launchpad in the centre of Reykjavík.

Designed by Guðjón Samúelsson, this modern concrete church was built in nationalistic style to resemble volcanic basalt columns. It dominates the skyline, a monument not only to God, but also to Iceland's belief that even a small country can have big dreams. Unless you are staying in one of the hotels nearby, you will almost certainly approach it up Skólavörðustígur, a road that takes off diagonally from the main shopping street. As you march up the hill, take time to admire the enticing galleries and bijoux boutiques that line both sides of the road, reflecting on how much artistic talent such a small country has produced... that is, if you can tear your eyes away from the gleaming white church.

Hallgrímskirkja's curves, columns and 73-metre (240ft) -high steeple are even more impressive from right up close. For further impact, head for the lift (daily May–Sept 9am– 8.30pm, Oct–Apr 9am– 4.30pm; charge) inside the main door, which sweeps you up to a **viewing platform** just above the clock. From here you get magnificent views not only of the city but also of the surrounding mountains, and a good sense of a community living comfortably alongside an often hostile environment. And, just to amplify the point, you may well get a blast of those strong winds, bringing cold air straight in from the snow-covered peaks.

Hallgrimskirkja

The interior of the church itself is very bare, as befits its Lutheran values, and there is not much to see except the magnificent organ, which is 15-metres (50ft) -high and has more than 5,000 pipes.

Just outside the church is a **statue of Leifur Eiríksson**, Iceland's greatest adventurer, who reached America long before Christopher Columbus. The statue, by Alexander Stirling Calder, was a gift from the US government to mark the Icelandic parliament's 1,000th anniversary in 1930. The explorer stands on a stylised longship, looking in the direction of America, still waiting for the full recognition his bravery deserves.

ARTISTS' HOMES

For more fascinating and enigmatic sculptures, cross the road to the **Einar Jónsson Museum** ❷ (Safn Einars Jónssonar; Eiríksgata 3; www.lej.is; Tue–Sun 10am–5pm; charge), the former home and studio of sculptor Einar Jónsson (1874–1954), a master of symbolism. Jónsson was virtually a recluse towards the end of his life, and many of the 100 or so ethereal marble pieces exhibited here are very melancholy in character. At the back of the building, on Freyjugata, the small sculpture garden is open year-round.

The former studio-home of another of the country's most celebrated artists is open to visitors in high summer. Continue down Njarðargata, then turn left onto Bergstaðastræti for the **Ásgrímur Jónsson Museum** ❸ (Bergstaðastræti 74; www.listasafn.is; July & Aug Mon–Fri 10am–2pm; charge). Iceland's first professional painter, Ásgrímur (1876–1958) was heavily influenced by the landscape and legends of his homeland. One room on the ground floor is left just as it was when he lived here, with

The stark Einar Jónsson Museum

his beloved piano taking centre stage, while upstairs there are examples of his often very colourful and emotional works of art.

LAUGAVEGUR: THE MAIN SHOPPING STREET

At the bottom of Skólavörðustígur is Reykjavík's main shopping street, **Laugavegur**. The name translates literally as 'Hot Spring Road', and it means what it says. This used to be the path to the hot pools in Laugardalur (see page 53), a green valley east of the city centre where Reykjavík's citizens once took their dirty laundry to wash.

Laugavegur is the nearest thing Iceland's capital has to a boulevard or avenue, with a mixture of internationally famous shops, local stores of all kinds and a wide selection of cafés, bars, restaurants and hotels. It's not exactly Oxford Street

Hand-knitted Icelandic jumpers

or Fifth Avenue, but a walk down here just window shopping and people watching is a great way to get an idea of what modern Icelandic life is all about. High fashion rubs shoulders with the highly practical, and local crafts hold their own alongside consumer goods from all over the globe. Where else in the world would you find traditional Icelandic sweaters and mud face-packs from the Blue Lagoon buddying up with Prada and Versace? The best of the shops are at the western end of Laugavegur, where it changes its name to Bankastræti, and then along Lækjargata and into the narrower little roads between the harbour and the City Hall. For more on shopping, see page 90.

As you walk down Bankastræti, **Government House** ❹ (Stjórnarráðshúsið; not open to the public) is to your right. This low, white, modest-looking affair is one of the oldest buildings in the country – built in 1761 as a prison, it now houses the offices of the prime minister. On the other side of Bankastræti, down the stairs of an old public toilet and in rude contrast to the quiet dignity of Government House, is the tiny **Icelandic Punk Museum** ❺ (Pönksafns Íslands; http://thepunkmuseum. is; Mon–Fri 10am–10pm, Sat–Sun noon–10pm; charge). A project of passion, here you can listen to music, play bass, guitar and drums, and learn about the history of punk in Iceland.

THE CULTURE HOUSE AND HARPA

For a quick cultural detour, head down Ingólfsstræti to Hverfisgata. To your left, standing on a hillock, is an imposing statue of Ingólfur Arnarson, the First Settler, who appears to be admiring the glinting Snæfellsjökull ice cap, 100km (62 miles) away to the north.

CULTURE HOUSE

To your right is the **Culture House** ❻ (Þjóðmenningarhús; Hverfisgata 15; www.culturehouse.is; May–mid-Sept daily 10am–5pm, mid-Sept–Apr Tue–Sun 10am–5pm; charge; ticket also valid for the National Museum). Until recently this was one of Reykjavík's most culturally important museums, home to a fascinating collection of medieval manuscripts. Now it's a rather disjointed hotchpotch of religious paintings, traditional handicrafts, contemporary art and stuffed animals, including one of the world's few remaining great auks (extinct since the last pair were bludgeoned to death in Iceland in 1844), which is worth a quick look. The 14th-century *Book of Skarð*, one of the most ornate Icelandic manuscripts, is still on display here, while five other medieval books have been moved to the Settlement Exhibition on Aðalstræti. The building itself, opened in 1909, was initially intended to be the National Library, and is considered one of Iceland's most beautiful pieces of home-grown architecture.

Next door is the **National Theatre** (1950), designed by state architect Guðjón Samúelsson, creator of Hallgrímskirkja, to resemble an Icelandic elf palace – an austere basalt rock from the outside, but which hides a magical world of colour, music, dance and song within.

HARPA

At the end of Ingólfsstræti, standing before you at the water's edge, is Iceland's latest cultural masterpiece, **Harpa** ❼ (tel: 528 5000; http://en.harpa.is; building open daily 8am–midnight, box office open Mon–Fri 9am–6pm, Sat–Sun 10am–6pm). Construction of the concert hall began a year before the 2008 crash, and for a while the half-finished shell seemed a doom-laden symbol of financial over-extension, and of the chaos and uncertainty facing the country. However, the government made a bold decision to forge ahead and complete the building, and today it is one of

⊙ BY THE BOOK

Iceland has always been a highly literate nation. It contributed the sagas to world culture, and on dark winter evenings in the ancient farmhouses, during the *kvöldvaka* ('evening wake'), it was traditional for one member of the family to read aloud while the others spun wool, sewed, knitted or made tools. A newer phenomenon is the *jólabókaflóð* ('Christmas book flood'), which originated during World War II. Paper was one of the few resources that wasn't rationed, so books became a popular gift when everything else was in short supply. In November every Icelandic household buys a flurry of newly published books, used to choose gifts for family and friends, which are opened and read on Christmas Eve. This little country publishes and sells more books per head than any other nation in the world: one in 10 Icelanders will publish a work of literature during their lifetime. In recognition of its staunch love of books and stories, Reykjavík was the first non-English-speaking city to be designated a Unesco City of Literature in 2011, a title that is held in perpetuity.

Harpa's chic interior

the city's highlights. The award-winning exterior, a glittering confection of steel and multicoloured glass designed by artist Ólafur Elíasson, reflects the city, sea and sky in a kaleidoscopic lightshow, which changes constantly with the daylight, weather and seasons. Inside its four concert halls are fitted out with state-of-the-art acoustic technology. From mid-June to August, there are 30-minute guided tours of the building on the hour (10am to 5pm; less frequently at other times; charge).

AUSTURVÖLLUR AND AÐALSTRÆTI

Laugavegur/Bankastræti ends at the busy dual-laned Lækjargata. Across the road is the concrete square **Lækjartorg**, a traditional Icelandic meeting-place. In days gone by, farmers driving their cattle to market commonly camped here. In modern times, it's the place to gather on drunken Friday nights after the bars close for burgers and waffles. Many of the city's main bus routes also call at the Lækjartorg stop.

AUSTURVÖLLUR

Take a short walk down Austurstræti, turning left to **Austurvöllur ❽** ('eastern field'). This small grassy square,

Grey-brick Parliament House

said to be where the First Viking Settler Ingólfur Arnarson grew his hay, is the true heart of the city. It may not look like much, but it is rich with symbols of nationhood. At its centre is a **statue of Jón Sigurðsson** (1811–1879), leader of the independence movement, who fought to free Iceland from Danish control. Jón gazes at the **Parliament House** 🟢 (Alþingishúsið) that he campaigned for all his life, a well-proportioned grey basalt mansion built a year after his death to house the ancient assembly. When parliament is sitting, debates among the country's 63 MPs can be observed from the public gallery; but, of course, you would need to understand Icelandic to appreciate the finer points of their arguments. Archaeological digs around the parliament building unearthed the first Viking Age industrial site found in Iceland: an iron smithy and fish- and wool-processing facilities.

Next door to Alþingishúsið is Reykjavík's neat white Lutheran cathedral, **Dómkirkjan** 🔟 (http://domkirkjan.is; Mon–Fri 10am–4pm; free), built in 1785. Although this is the bona fide headquarters of the country's official religion, the little cathedral is often mistaken for a simple church by visitors, who assume that ostentatious Hallgrímskirkja is where the Bishop of Iceland hangs out. Completely overshadowed by its flashy cousin, the cathedral neverthe-less has an understated charm of its own. Behind its plain facade, the trim, galleried interior has a ceiling studded with golden stars, and arched windows that bathe the place in clean, clear northern light.

Along the eastern side of Austurvöllur is Hotel Borg, the city's first hotel, built in 1930 by a circus strongman.

⊙ ICELAND'S MEDIEVAL MANUSCRIPTS

Iceland's priceless collection of medieval manuscripts, dat-ing back to the 12th century, are full of details of life in Iceland and northern Europe from the time of the Vikings onwards. Their survival is largely thanks to the tireless work of Árni Magnússon (1663–1730), librarian, historian and antiquarian. Árni conducted a 10-year census of Iceland, during which time he begged, bought and borrowed all the Icelandic books and manuscripts he could get his hands on, whisking them away to Denmark for safe keeping. Tragically many were then lost when his house burned down in the Great Fire of Copenhagen in 1728. Those that survived were a source of constant dispute between the Danes and the Icelanders, until the most precious were finally returned to Iceland in 1971. Around 1,400 manu-scripts and manuscript fragments still remain at the Arna-magnæan Institute in Copenhagen, while the rest are held at Iceland's Árni Magnússon Institute. A handful are on display to the public in Reykjavík at the Culture House and the Settle-ment Exhibition. The House of Icelandic Studies (Hús íslenskra fræða), due to open in 2021, will be a research centre for Iceland-dic language, literature and history, and will hopefully display the manuscripts in all their glory to curious visitors.

AÐALSTRÆTI

Just west of Austurvöllur is Aðalstræti, the city's oldest street. Opposite No. 9 Aðalstræti is a freshwater well, discovered by chance during road works in 1992, and believed to be where the First Settler, Ingólfur Arnarson, drew his drinking water. **Number 10 Aðalstræti ⓫** (daily 10am–5pm; charge; ticket also valid for The Settlement Exhibition), the oldest surviving house in Reykjavík, dates from 1762 and once belonged to the High Sheriff of Iceland, Skúli Magnússon. When Reykjavík was little more than a town in the mid-eighteenth century, Skúli took it upon himself to set up local crafts and industries and bring in new skills, and is now regarded as the city's founder. The house is owned by Reykjavík City Museum, and contains two small exhibitions, 'Reykjavík 1918' and 'A Town of Turf Houses', examining Reykjavík's metamorphosis from provincial village to capital city.

A far older – albeit ruined – home lies below street level in the **Settlement Exhibition ⓬** (Landnámssýning; Aðalstræti 16; www.reykjavik871.is; daily 9am–6pm; charge; ticket also valid for Number 10 Aðalstræti). This excellent underground museum, built around the remains of an excavated Viking Age farmhouse, does an

Number 10 Aðalstræti

imaginative job of exploring how Reykjavík might have looked in Viking times. A modest turf wall belonging to the farm presents a tantalising puzzle: it lies underneath a layer of volcanic ash dated to AD 871... three years before the official settlement date. Four of Iceland's priceless medieval manuscripts – *Landnámabók*, *Íslendingabók*, *Kjalnesingasaga* and *Jónsbók*, which detail the country's settlement and early laws – have been placed in a small side exhibition here. They sit alongside the *Bill of Purchase for Reykjavík* (1615), detailing the sale of the land on which the city stands by a widow to the governor of Iceland, acting on behalf of the Danish king. The price was the equivalent of 60 cows.

TJÖRNIN AND AROUND

ON THE LAKE SHORES

Return to Austurvöllur and slip between the parliament and the cathedral to behold the lovely city-centre lake, **Tjörnin** ⑬ ('The Pond'), favoured by over 40 species of birds. You'll find ducks and swans here even in the depths of winter: geothermal water is pumped into the northeastern corner to leave an ice-free place for them to swim. Noticeboards along the footpath that runs around the lake explain all about the various species, including their migration and feeding patterns.

On the northern bank is **Reykjavík City Hall** ⑭ (Raðhús), a key example of 20th-century Icelandic architecture. The modern glass-and-concrete construction was designed to link the people with their politicians, and the city buildings with the lake. It contains a café, a large 3D map of Iceland and the main **Visit Reykjavík tourist office** (tel: 411 6040; www.visitreykjavik. is; daily 8am–8pm), accessed by a wooden walkway.

National Gallery of Iceland

Alongside the lake to the west are some fine old mansions, backed by **Hólavallagarður**, the largest 19th-century cemetery in Iceland. It's the post-life home of many notable Icelanders, including Jón Sigurðsson, hero of Iceland's independence movement, and Jóhannes Kjarval, the country's best-loved painter.

On the eastern shore is the **National Gallery of Iceland 15** (Listasafn Íslands; Fríkirkjuvegur 7; www.listasafn.is; mid-May–Sept daily 10am–5pm, Oct–mid-May Tue–Sun 11am–5pm; charge). The building was originally designed by Guðjón Samúelsson, of Hallgrímskirkja fame, as an ice house: blocks of ice cut from the frozen lake were stored there, and then used to pack and preserve the fish catch that was sold and transported to Britain. The gallery has a fine permanent collection of 19th- and 20th-century Icelandic and foreign art, including works by the country's first professional artist, Ásgrímur Jónsson (1876–1958), and international stars Picasso and Munch. However, much of the collection is hidden away in storage, as there is limited gallery space inside the little ice house, but exhibitions are changed frequently to give the works an airing.

⊙ REYKJAVÍK CITY CARD

Before exploring the city, consider investing in a Reykjavík City Card. It can be purchased from tourist offices, some museums and many hotels and hostels, for a cost of ISK3,800 (€30) for 24 hours, ISK5,400 (€43) for 48 hours and ISK6,500 (€52) for 72 hours. The card gives access to the following list of museums and galleries, and all the city's swimming pools. It also entitles the holder to free travel on the city buses (Strætó) and a free ferry trip to Viðey island. Discounts are offered on some tours and in selected shops and restaurants – see visitreykjavik.is for the latest.

Reykjavík Art Museum (Kjarvalsstaðir, Ásmundarsafn, Hafnarhús)

The Culture House

Number 10 Aðalstræti

The Settlement Exhibition

National Gallery of Iceland

National Museum of Iceland

Museum of Photography

Maritime Museum

Reykjavík Zoo and Family Park

Árbæjarsafn open-air museum

Gerðarsafn (in Kopavogur)

THE NATIONAL MUSEUM OF ICELAND

A 15-minute walk south of the gallery is the must-see **National Museum of Iceland** ⑯ (Þjóðminjasafn Íslands; Hringbraut, Suðurgata 1, junction with Hringbraut; www.thjodminjasafn.is; May–mid-Sept daily 10am–5pm, mid-Sept–Apr Tue–Sun 10am–5pm; charge; ticket also valid for the Culture House). The museum's permanent exhibition, 'The Making of a Nation', is gripping stuff, tracing Iceland's history from the Viking settlement to the present day. It begins with the ship in which the First Settlers crossed the ocean to their new home, and ends upstairs in a modern airport. The early medieval section is the most absorbing: a fascinating display details DNA testing on the teeth of the First Settlers to determine their origins, and unique artefacts from the period include the elaborately carved 12th-century Valþjófsstaður church door, depicting a dragon-slaying knight and his faithful lion friend. The later history concentrates on the economic development of the country and its growing political emergence after centuries of foreign rule. Particularly interesting is the census of 1703, the first to record the entire population of Iceland, along with their livestock and details of their living conditions. Allow a couple of hours.

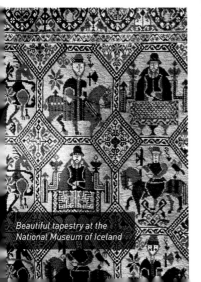

Beautiful tapestry at the National Museum of Iceland

NORDIC HOUSE

Between the National Museum and Reykjavík's domestic airport is **Nordic House** ⑰ (Norræna Húsið; Sæmundargata 11; www.nordichouse.is; exhibition spaces daily 10am–5pm, Wed until 9pm; charge for some exhibitions), designed by the renowned Finnish architect Alvar Aalto in 1968. Its purpose is to cultivate and strengthen cultural ties between the Nordic countries. It contains a library, concert hall, exhibition spaces, design shop and upmarket 'New Nordic' restaurant, and has an ongoing programme of events.

Winter temperatures

Iceland isn´t as cold as it sounds. The Gulf Stream keeps temperatures moderate all year round. Even in winter it doesn't snow much in Reykjavík. Average January temperatures are around zero, higher than those in New York.

THE HARBOURS AND THE SEA

HAFNARSTRÆTI

Back in the city centre, two streets away from Austurvöllur, **Hafnarstræti** ⑱ ('harbour street') was once the old quayside. During World War I, the land was extended northwards by dumping gravel and sand in the sea to form a new harbourside, Tryggvagata; which was extended again into today's harbourfront Geirsgata. Hafnarstræti is a pleasant part of town in summer, with a mixture of cafés, bars, shops and galleries nestled inside some quaint old wood and corrugated-iron buildings. The listed **Fálkahúsið** (Nos 1–3), for example, perches on the site where the king of Denmark once kept his prize falcons: two carved wooden birds on the roof commemorate the fact. No. 18, now housing Zimsen's bar, was an 18th-century fish warehouse.

TRYGGVAGATA

On Tryggvagata, from east to west, are Kolaportið, Hafnarhús, the library and Volcano House, all of interest to visitors. **Kolaportið Flea Market ⓳** (Tryggvagata 19; www.kolaportid. is; Sat–Sun 11am–5pm), in the old customs building, is a small but cheerful occasion selling second-hand clothes, books and odds and ends. The food section is a must for anyone curious about traditional fishy treats, like *harðfiskur* (dried fish), *hákarl* (cured shark) and *síld* (pickled herring). On the front of the new customs building nearby, a colourful mural depicts the busy life of the harbour in mosaic form.

Hafnarhús ⓴ (Tryggvagata 17; http://artmuseum.is/ hafnarhus; daily 10am–5pm, Thu until 10pm; charge), one of three galleries belonging to the Reykjavík Art Museum, is situated in the stylishly renovated former warehouse of the Port of Reykjavík. Scattered across six large exhibition halls, you will find some extraordinary contemporary works by 20th- and 21st-century artists, as well as permanent works by internationally renowned Icelandic pop artist, Erró (1932–), who donated around 4,000 paintings, sculptures and collages to the city. Your ticket is valid for 24 hours and will also get you into the Kjarvalsstaðir and Ásmundursafn art galleries (see pages 52 and 54).

Next door, the city library has an interesting little **photo museum ㉑** (Tryggvagata 15; www.ljosmyndasafnreykjavikur. is; Mon–Thu 10am–6pm, Fri 11am–6pm, Sat–Sun 1–5pm; charge) on the top floor, with changing exhibitions showing off some of the six million photographs in its collection.

Continuing west, a very different kind of visual experience awaits at **Volcano House ㉒** (Eldstöðin; Tryggvagata 11; www.

volcanohouse.is; daily 9am–10pm, shows on the hour 10am–9pm; charge). Two short documentary films (total run-time 53 minutes) show dramatic footage of the 1973 Heimaey eruption and the 2010 Eyjafjallajökull eruption, supported by a small exhibition on Iceland's unique geology. Together they are a good introduction to the immense subterranean forces that constantly reshape the country.

Kolaportið Flea Market

THE 'OLD HARBOUR'

Tryggvagata ends outside the Volcano House – cross the double lanes of traffic on busy Geirsgata and head down Suðurbugt to the glinting water. To your left and right sprawls Reykjavík's 'Old Harbour' (so-called because newer sections exist to the west), busy with boats and activity: small pleasure crafts, trawlers bringing in their catch, perhaps the hulking grey shape of an Icelandic coastguard vessel, with the blue, white and red national flag slashed across its bow, or a replica sailing ship paying Iceland a visit. Set apart from the other boats, and looking defiant and even a little threatening, are the highly controversial whaling ships, recognisable by their black hulls and a red H (for 'hvalur' or 'whale') on their funnels.

If you follow the Sculpture and Shore Walk path left – past the colourful teal buildings holding a great choice of cafés and seafood restaurants – you will come to Ægisgarður,

Enjoying an Elding whale-watching tour

where three companies offer much more conservation-friendly 2.5 to 3hr **whale-watching tours** ㉓ – Elding (tel: 519 5000; www.elding.is), Special Tours (tel: 560 8800; www.specialtours.is) and Whale Safari (tel: 497 0000; www.whalesafari.is). Between mid-May and mid-August, boats also sail past the tiny island of Lundey or Akurey, so passengers can get a good look at the puffins.

In summertime, Elding also runs the ferry (tel: 533 5055; mid-May to September from Ægisgarður pier, year-round departures from Skarfabakki pier) to the island of **Viðey** ㉔, a haunting and historically significant place full of tussocked grass and soughing wind. The bird life is prolific, and there are some impressive basalt columns on the isthmus at the centre of the island, as well as modern sculptures including Yoko Ono's *Imagine Peace Tower*, which lights up the sky on significant dates. The ferry takes less than 10 minutes, and Viðey is small enough to stroll around in an hour or two.

GRANDI

Following the pedestrian Sculpture & Shore Walk path further west brings you to Grandi, a rather ugly and industrial part of the harbour, still used by fishing boats and small passenger vessels, and for ship repairs. At first glance, the setting is not promising, but over the past five years, many trendy shops, bistros, studios and tourist attractions have been relocating here. The newest is **Aurora Reykjavík** ㉕ (Grandagarður 2; http://aurorareykjavik.is; daily 9am–9pm;

⊘ PUFFINS

The colourful Atlantic puffin – with its large, stripy beak and bright orange legs and feet – is a great favourite with visitors. Puffins are highly sociable, often standing about in groups and nesting in large colonies. They fish together, too, forming wide rafts out to sea, diving to depths of 60 metres (200ft) in search of their main food, sand eels.

Both parents share child-rearing responsibilities. They dig burrows deep into the cliff sides, and stand guard over their precious single egg, rarely travelling far from the colony while raising their young.

Traditionally, puffins are hunted for food in Iceland, fished out of the air with huge nets. They produce a dark meat, like duck but less fatty, often served with a blueberry sauce. However, concerns over declining colonies have led to a hunting ban in the Vestmannaeyjar, once the capital of puffins and puffin-hunting.

charge), a small exhibition of film and photos that offers summer visitors a chance to learn about the Northern Lights, invisible in the 24-hour daylight.

Just up the road by the roundabout is the **Saga Museum ㉖** (Sögusafnið; www.sagamuseum.is; daily 10am–6pm; charge), a mixture of Madame Tussauds and a film set for a movie about marauding Vikings. Dramatic tableaux with life-size models introduce you to Iceland's best-known historical figures and saga characters – Snorri Sturluson, Erik the Red, Leifur Eiríksson and the rest – and often cover the gory ways in which these people died as well. You are led around the dioramas by an audioguide, which takes around half an hour.

Also out at Grandi is **Bryggjan Brugghús** (http://bryggjan-brugghus.is; 11am–1am daily), Iceland's first microbrewery and a great place to sample the country's current craze for craft beer. Next door, the worthwhile **Reykjavík Maritime Museum ㉗** (Sjóminjasafnið á Reykjavík; Grandagarður 8; http://borgarsogusafn.is; daily 10am–5pm; charge), based in an old fish-freezing plant, reopened in 2018 after a much-needed revamp. The first of its two permanent exhibitions, 'Fish & Folk', explores Iceland's fishing industry and the crucial part cod has played in the survival of the nation, as well as delving into the dangers of life at sea. A compelling combination of photos, artefacts and games follow the codfish on its journey from the sea to the dinner table. The second permanent exhibition – on the first floor – takes a fascinating look at how items were recovered from the Dutch merchant ship *Melckmeyt* ('The Milkmaid'), which was shipwrecked off Flatey island in 1659. There are daily guided tours aboard the coastguard ship *Óðinn* at 11am, 1pm, 2pm and 3pm.

Right at the end of Grandagarður, in a former fishmeal factory, is Marshall House, a newly opened centre for visual art. It contains three Icelandic artistic institutions. On the first floor is **The Living Art Museum** ㉘ (Nýlistasafnið or Nýló; Grandagarður 20; www.nylo.is; Tue–Sun noon–6pm, Thu until 9pm; free), an artist-run not-for-profit art gallery committed to providing a forum for the most innovative and cutting-edge art in the country. Since it was founded in 1978, it has been building up an impressive permanent collection, helped by the fact that all artists who join the association must donate an example of their work. There are six to eight different contemporary exhibitions every year, as well as a programme of performance art, readings and concerts. Upstairs, **Gallery Kling & Bang** (Wed–Sun noon–6pm, Thu until 9pm; free) is an alliance of artists who invite established and emerging creators from home and abroad to exhibit works in their gallery space. The top floor of the building contains the private studio of Ólafur Elíasson, who created Harpa's glinting facade.

Punctuating the end of Grandi like a fullstop, the outdoor art installation **þúfa** ㉙ (2013) by artist Ólöf Nordal stands on a small cape. A spiralling pathway runs up a grassy hillock, which is topped by

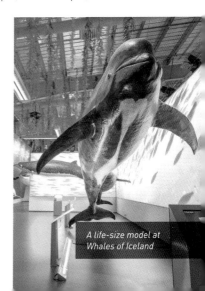

A life-size model at Whales of Iceland

a shack for wind-drying fish. A reference to simpler times and the industry on which the city was built, the artwork offers visitors a slice of peace and contemplation, plus fabulous views back over Reykjavík and out to the surrounding mountains.

Curl round on Fiskislóð to **Whales of Iceland** ㉚ (Fiskislóð 23–25; http://whalesoficeland.is; daily 10am–5pm; charge) to learn about these amazing creatures. Whalesong accompanies you through this multimedia exhibition, lit as though underwater and containing 23 life-size models of the various whale species around Iceland's coast.

Bus 14 runs from Fiskislóð and Grandagarður back to the city centre.

EASTWARDS TO LAUGARDALUR

Laugardalur – a green geothermal valley – was where Reykjavík's citizens once took their dirty laundry to wash in the natural hot springs. Today, Reykjavík still makes use of the valley's subterranean heat: it supplies the city with around eight percent of its hot water. Laugardalur is also Reykjavík's main recreation area, with the national football stadium and assorted sports facilities gridding together around a large park and zoo of local animals. You can get to Laugardalur on foot (approximately 4km/2.5 miles from the city centre); via city bus No. 14; or by hiring a bicycle and heading east along the lovely coastal pedestrian/cycling path.

ALONG THE COASTAL PATH

Four hundred metres (550yds) east of Harpa concert hall is Jón Gunnar Árnason's distinctive stainless-steel sculpture, *Sólfar* ㉛ (Sun Voyager; 1986). Resembling a silver Viking longboat, the structure symbolises light, hope and the promise of undiscovered lands. It occupies an impressive spot looking out over the sea, with great views of Mt Esja on the other side of the bay.

Just beyond the Sólfar sculpture, you might want to take a detour inland up the unfortunately dull and ugly road Snorrabraut to visit three very different museums. **The Icelandic Phallological Museum ㉜** (Íslenzka Reðasafn; Laugavegur 116; http://phallus.is; daily June–Aug 9am–6pm, Sept–May 10am–6pm; charge) displays over 200 penises from almost every Icelandic mammal, including a 95-year-old human who bequeathed his member to the museum.

Tales from Iceland ㉝ (Snorrabraut 37; www.talesfromiceland.is; daily 9am–5pm; charge) is a self-styled 'video museum', with large screens showing three- to four-minute films about Iceland's nature, culture and people. The engaging and informative footage comes from local news clips and visitor vignettes, and will easily absorb you for an hour.

The Icelandic Phallological Museum

Höfði House

A little further inland is **Kjarvalsstaðir** ㉞ (Municipal Gallery; Flókagata 24; http://artmuseum.is/kjarvalsstadir; daily 10am–5pm; charge), whose exhibition halls are usually well worth the trek. Half the gallery is dedicated to the huge, colourful, often abstract landscapes by Icelandic artist Jóhannes Kjarval (1885–1972), while the other half houses visiting exhibitions. Your ticket is valid for 24 hours and will also get you into Hafnarhús and Ásmundursafn (see pages 44 and 54). One street away, Háteigskirkja (Háteigsvegur; Tue–Fri 9am–4pm) is an unusual little church, with four sharp black spires that look like witches' hats.

Back on the coast, the stately **Höfði House** ㉟ (closed to the public) stands in splendid isolation in a grassy square. This out-of-the-way building became the focus of the entire world's media in 1986, when President Reagan and Soviet leader Mikhail Gorbachev met here to discuss global disarmament and the ending of the Cold War. There is no record of the two world leaders being troubled by ghosts, but when Höfði served as the British Embassy in the 1950s, the resident envoy was so freaked out by 'bumps in the night' that he made the British Foreign Office sell the building back to the Icelandic government.

A kilometre east is the peaceful **Sigurjón Ólafsson Museum 36** (Laugarnestangi 70; http://lso.is; mid-May–mid-Sept daily 1–5pm, mid-Sept–Nov, Feb–mid-May Sat–Sun 2–5pm, closed Dec and Jan; charge), dedicated to the sculptor whose beautiful home and studio this was. In addition to the art collection, there is a small family-run café with a lovely sea view. The museum puts on popular concerts at 8.30pm on Tuesdays in summer. Opening hours are generally decided season by season, so double check times on the website before making a special trip out here.

Just east of the museum, a year-round ferry runs to the island of Viðey (see page 46) from Skarfabakki wharf at Sundahöfn harbour, where the cruise ships dock.

LAUGARDALUR

Inland is Laugardalur, a green valley that serves as the capital's sports and recreation area, containing the national soccer stadium, running tracks, athletics fields, a sports hall, a large swimming pool, camping ground and ice-skating rink (winter only), as well as a park, botanical garden and petting zoo. The pool complex **Laugardalslaug 37** (Sundlaugavegur 30; Mon–Fri 6.30am–10pm, Sat & Sun 8am–10pm; charge) is the biggest in the city, with a 50-metre (164ft) open-air thermal pool, a large children's pool with waterslides, and hot pots, sauna and steam room. The **Botanical Gardens 38** (www.grasagardur.is; daily May–Sept 10am–10pm, Oct–Apr 10am–3pm; free) have an impressive – for this latitude at least! – collection of 5,000 plants, and a pleasant summer café. Nearby, there is a good playground with mini rides (tiny diggers, bouncy castle, paddleboats etc) at the **Family Park and Reykjavík Zoo 39** (www.mu.is; daily 10am–5pm, until 6pm in summer; charge), which contains domestic farm animals, Arctic foxes, mink, reindeers, seals and a small cold-water aquarium. Feeding times for the various animals are posted up at the entrance.

On the edge of Laugardalur is **Ásmundarsafn** ㊵ (Ásmundur Sveinsson Sculpture Museum; Sigtún 105; http://artmuseum. is/asmundarsafn; daily May–Sept 10am–5pm, Oct–Apr 1–5pm; charge). Ásmundur Sveinsson (1893–1982) was a pioneer of Icelandic sculpture, who firmly believed art belonged to the masses – the masses, however, often found his abstract works far too controversial and challenging for their tastes. Influenced by his tutor Carl Milles, ancient Greek statues and the revolutionary Cubist movement, Ásmundur's early sculptures depict characters from Icelandic sagas and folk tales, or the people of Iceland hard at work, and are massive and earthy in style, while later pieces became ever lighter and

Al-fresco works at the Ásmundarsafn

more abstract. Several works stand in the garden of the artist's self-built studio-home, so you can get a taster before heading inside. Your ticket is valid for 24 hours and will also get you into Hafnarhús and Kjarvalsstaðir (see pages 44 and 52).

ÁRBÆJARSAFN

A short bus or taxi journey further east takes you to **Árbæjarsafn ❹** (Arbær Open-Air Museum; daily June–Aug 10am–5pm, Sept–May 1pm–5pm; charge). The farm on this spot dates back to at least the 13th century, and for many years was a popular rest stop for people travelling between the city and the countryside. After falling into disrepair, it was chosen in 1957 to be the site of an open-air museum. Around 20 buildings of historical interest were moved here from other parts of Reykjavík and further afield to form a kind of village. Together they give visitors a strong sense of how life was lived in 19th-century Iceland, when rural Reykjavík was on the cusp of transformation. The buildings include turf-roofed homesteads, a turf-roofed church and shops and workshops such as a blacksmith's, shoemaker's and old-fashioned sweet shop. Children can try their hand at traditional games and helpful staff, dressed in period clothes, will explain what's what. There is also an excellent guided tour in English at 1pm daily.

Turf houses

In Europe, turf houses date back to the Iron Age. Iceland is unusual in that turf was used to construct all kinds of buildings (houses, barns, churches), for all classes of society, from Settlement times right into the 20th century. Most of Iceland's turf houses now belong to the National Museum of Iceland.

PERLAN, ÖSKJUHLÍÐ AND NAUTHÓLSVÍK

When you first drove from Keflavík airport into the capital, you may have caught sight of a bizarre futuristic-looking structure with a glittering dome, perched on top of a hillside on the south side of the city. This is Perlan (The Pearl), and it is houses the city's hot water supply. Over five million gallons

⊙ ICELAND'S FAVOURITE ARTIST

Jóhannes Sveinsson Kjarval (1885–1972) was a legend in his own lifetime, rising from humble roots to become the figure-head of Iceland's great cultural renaissance. Born into biting poverty, Kjarval was sent to the remote northeast at the age of four to be raised by fisherman, spending every free moment painting. At the age of 27, his fellow fishermen and trade-union members clubbed together to send him to study at the Royal Danish Academy of Fine Arts in Copenhagen.

Kjarval was a prolific artist, and his legacy includes thousands of doodles, sketches, drawings and paintings. His personal style mixes impressionist, expressionist, cubist, abstract and even absurdist elements with a splash of something quintessentially Icelandic. He is best known for his paintings of Icelandic nature, which capture the restless and uncanny feel of the country's landscape like nothing else: in his work, every rock and piece of lichen seems to throb with a near-hallucinatory lifeforce.

Kjarval is celebrated with his own municipal art gallery (Kjarvalsstaðir – see page 52) and he appears on the front of the 2000-krónur banknote, sporting a natty hat. The back of the note shows two of his works, *Flugþrá* ('Yearning for Flight') and *Kona og blóm* ('Woman and Flowers').

of geothermally heated water are stored in its rounded tanks.

Perlan is not just functional, but a visitor destination in its own right. **Perlan – Wonders of Iceland**  (https://perlan. is; daily 8am–8pm, last admissions 7pm; charge) is the city's newest and most ambitious entertainment project, using cutting-edge technology to bring Iceland's geological marvels to life. Visitors

The sun compass of Iceland at Perlan – Wonders of Iceland

see, hear and feel the power of volcanoes, earthquakes and geothermal energy, walk through a 100-metre (110yd) -long ice cave, built with over 350 tonnes of snow, and watch whales swimming in a virtual aquarium. A 360-degree viewing deck sits on top of the hot water tanks, giving fantastic views of Reykjavík and the surrounding area. At the time of writing, a planetarium was also being constructed at the site. A free shuttle bus runs from Harpa concert hall in the city centre to Perlan every half hour between 9am and 5.30pm.

Öskjuhlíð, the hill on which Perlan sits, used to be a barren spot, littered with trenches, bunkers and fuel stores built during World War II by the British army. Today it is green and leafy, thanks to an ambitious tree-planting scheme, and is a popular place to take a break from urban life. Walking tracks and bike routes crisscross its slopes, and the hillside is a favourite sunbathing spot when the weather allows.

The Northern Lights glow green above Reykjavík

Heading 1.5km (1 mile) downhill through the pine and birch trees to the southern coast brings you to another little jewel – Reykjavík's purpose-built **geothermal beach** ⓭ (www.nautholsvik.is; mid-May–mid-Aug daily 10am–7pm, mid-Aug–mid-May Mon and Wed 11am–2pm and 5–8pm, Fri 11am–2pm, Sat 11am–4pm; free in summer) at Nauthólsvík. This pocket-sized crescent of golden sand is a slice of happiness on a sunny day, when people flock here to catch the rays and bathe outdoors in the bay, which is heated (by water from Perlan) to an average temperature of 17°C (63°F) in summer. The geothermal hot pots reach a toastier 30°C to 39°C (86°F to 95°F).

SELTJARNARNES

When the hectic pace of city life gets too much, you can walk, cycle or take bus No. 11 to the western end of the peninsula.

The headland of Seltjarnarnes is a beautiful little spot with a real feeling of wildness, despite being so close to the centre. There's not much here except Seltjarnarnes golf club, Bakkatjörn lake and a path to **Grótta lighthouse and nature reserve** (closed May–mid-July due to bird nesting), from where you can watch the seabirds and the waves that come

⊙ THE NORTHERN LIGHTS

The bewitching *aurora borealis*, commonly known as the Northern Lights, flashes, flickers and pulses across the winter sky like silent fireworks. This eerie green lightshow, sometimes tinged with purples, pinks and reds, has been the source of many a high-latitude superstition: the Vikings, for example, believed it was the Valkyries riding across the sky. The scientific explanation is no less astonishing. The lights are actually caused by streams of charged particles – 'solar wind' – that flare into space from our sun. When solar wind comes into contact with the Earth's magnetic field, it is drawn towards the poles, where its electrical charge agitates particles of oxygen and nitrogen in the atmosphere, making them glow.

In Iceland, the lights can be seen between September/October and March/April, with midnight being the most likely time to see them... but as with all natural phenomena, there's no timetable and sightings are not guaranteed. You don't need to go out into the countryside, as the lights are clearly visible from darker areas of the city. Choose a cold, clear, moonless night; then look heavenwards and hope. To help your search, the Icelandic Meteorological Office has a Northern Lights forecast (en. vedur.is/weather/forecasts/aurora), or you could download the My Aurora Forecast app (for Android and iPhone).

pounding in from the Atlantic. The path is only walkable at low tide – keep an eye on the water, otherwise you could get stranded!

GREATER REYKJAVÍK

Outside the immediate city centre, the wider suburbs hide a few attractions that are worth a visit, depending on your interests and how much time you have available to explore.

KÓPAVOGUR

A residential suburb of Reykjavík, **Kópavogur** ⑮ has a couple of interesting cultural sights, including the only museum in Iceland dedicated to a female artist. **Gerðarsafn** (Hamraborg 4; https://gerdarsafn.kopavogur.is; Tue–Sun 11am–5pm; charge) celebrates the life and work of sculptor Gerður Helgadóttir (1928–1975), drawing on some 1,400 esoteric works in concrete, plaster, clay and iron, along with stained glass and mosaics, that were donated to the municipality by her family. Gerður also designed the stained-glass windows of **Kópavogskirkja** (1963), a distinctive church standing just at the end of the road.

Across the street, the cute little **Natural History Museum** (Náttúrufræðistofa Kópavogs; Hamraborg 6a; https://natkop.kopavogur.is; Mon–Thu 9am–6pm, Fri & Sat 11am–5pm; free) displays geological and zoological exhibits from Icelandic nature. Ask at the desk for a guide in English, as all of the signage is in Icelandic.

Kópavogur is also home to **Smáralind** (www.smaralind.is; Mon–Fri 11am–7pm, Thu to 9pm, Sat 11am–6pm, Sun 1–6pm), the second-largest shopping mall in Iceland with around 90 shops and restaurants and a cinema.

Smáralind

City bus No. 1 runs from the centre of Reykjavík southeast to Kópavogur.

MOSFELLSBÆR

The green and hilly **Mosfellsbær** 46 district lies 12km (7 miles) east of Reykjavík. Its main interest for visitors is **Gljúfrasteinn** (www.gljufrasteinn.is; June–Aug daily 9am–5pm, Sept, Oct, Apr, May Tue–Sun 10am–4pm, Nov–Mar Tue–Fri 10am–4pm; charge). This is the former home of Iceland's most important modern literary figure, Halldór Kiljan Laxness (1902–98), winner of the 1955 Nobel Prize for Literature. Laxness was a prolific author, writing 62 works in 68 years. He was also a controversial one, portraying the dark underside of rural life, using uncouth street language and sometimes even making up new words – all considered highly unpatriotic acts. His best-known creation,

Hafnarfjörður by night

Bjartur, the protagonist of *Independent People*, is stubborn, infuriating and hamstrung by debt – a sly caricature of the 'archetypal' Icelander. For directions on how to reach the museum, see the website.

The river Varmá runs through Mosfellsbær, and once drove the machinery of the 19th-century Álafoss woollen mill. Knitters and crocheters will be drawn like moths to a flame to the **Álafoss factory shop** (Álafossvegur 23; https://alafoss.is; Mon–Fri 8am–8pm, Sat & Sun 9am–8pm), where the full range of *lopi*, *léttlopi* and *plötulopi* is for sale.

Fans of Sigur Rós might be interested to know that the band's recording studio is based in the district's old swimming pool, chosen for its acoustics. It's definitely worth bringing your swimsuit for a visit to the modern pool, **Lágafellslaug** (Lækjarhlíð 1a; Mon–Fri 6.30am–9.30pm, Sat & Sun 8am–7pm; charge), which has an especially good toddlers' section.

Mosfellsbær is a 20-minute bus ride (No. 15) from Hlemmur bus stop.

HAFNARFJÖRÐUR

The old town of **Hafnarfjörður** ④⑦, surrounded by the craggy Búrfell lava field, was once one of Iceland's most important ports. Today it's practically a suburb of Reykjavík, although it does still manage to hang on to its own personality in spite of the city's slow engulfing sprawl. You can get a sense of the town's past at **Hafnarfjörður Museum** (www.visithafnarfjordur.is), based across four separate sites: the two main buildings are Pakkhúsið (Vesturgata 8; June–Aug daily 11am–5pm, rest of year Sat–Sun 11am–5pm; charge), which takes visitors

⊘ GAME OF THRONES

Game of Thrones, HBO's smash TV series, has been credited with doubling the number of visitors to Iceland between 2011, when it first aired, and 2018. Scenes from the Vale, the Wall and Beyond the Wall were filmed at various sites across the country, and fans have been flocking here to follow in the footsteps of Jon Snow, Ygritte and the wildlings. Iceland's harsh glacier-filled landscape is the perfect setting for the savage northern wastes of Westeros; and of course the country itself is infused with the spirit of the bloodthirsty medieval sagas, where families are torn apart by ferocious feuds and brutal battles. Committed fans can take a specialist eight-hour *Game of Thrones* tour from Reykjavík: providers include Gray Line (grayline.is) and Arctic Adventures (adventures.is). More casual viewers can still see some of the locations on bus trips to Þingvellir National Park, where Arya and the Hound made their futile journey to the Bloody Gate; the black-sand beaches around Vík on the south coast, which were used for scenes at Eastwatch-by-the-Sea; and Kirkjufell, on Snæfellsnes peninsula, which is the 'mountain like an arrowhead' from season 7. Filming for Season 8 had just wrapped at the time of writing, mostly taking place around Skaftafell on the south coast.

Cruise ships

Reykjavík is increasingly popular as a cruise-ship destination. Ships dock at Sundahöfn harbour (east of the city centre), and bring 144,000 visitors a year to the city.

on an interesting canter through the town's history, and amuses children with a little toy museum; and next door Sívertsen's House (Sívertsens-Hús; June–Aug daily 11am–5pm; charge), the 19th-century home of local bigwig, Bjarni Sívertsen.

The cool, white **Hafnarborg Centre of Culture and Fine Art** (Strandgata 34; www.hafnarborg.is; Wed–Mon noon–5pm; free), a genuine highlight of the town, offers art exhibitions and musical events, as well as a peaceful coffee shop.

Hafnarfjörður is well known for its 'hidden people' – elves, trolls and other supernatural creatures said to live in the surrounding lava. **Hellisgerði Park** (Nönnustígur; open all year; free) is a *huldufólk* hotspot. In mid-June, Fjörukráin (Viking Village, Strandgata 50; www.fjorukrain.is), the nation's only Viking guesthouse and restaurant, is the centre of a small Viking festival (Víkingahátíð), with a medieval marketplace, lamb roast, music and mock battles.

Hafnarfjörður is a 20-minute bus-ride from Reykjavík centre on city bus No. 1.

DAY TRIPS BY BUS

If you are in the Reykjavík area for anything more than a couple of days, venturing out of the city is a must. You could hire a car, but there is also an amazing variety of convenient tour-bus day trips. Two of the biggest tour-bus companies are Reykjavík Excursions (tel: 580 5400, www.re.is)

and Gray Line (tel: 540 1313, grayline.is). The most popular excursions are to see the sights of the Golden Circle or to chill out at the Blue Lagoon. Active types can arrange to go horse-riding, hiking, fishing, caving, kayaking, rafting, scuba-diving, glacier-walking, snowmobiling or swooping over Iceland's volcanoes and ice-floes in a private plane or helicopter – all possible as day trips from Reykjavík.

The following is just a small selection of the many possibilities on offer.

THE BLUE LAGOON

Iceland's most famous tourist attraction, the **Blue Lagoon** ⓭ (Bláa Lónið; tel: 420 8800; www.bluelagoon. com; daily July–mid-Aug 7am–midnight, June 7am–11pm, Jan–May and mid-Aug–Sept 8am–10pm, Oct–Dec 8am–9pm; charge) is a dreamy, steamy outdoor spa complex that epitomises the country's faintly unearthly reputation. Little wooden bridges criss-cross its blue-white waters, which are a toasty 37–40°C (98–104°F) all year round. The complex – expanded in 2018 – also contains a spa treatment area, two restaurants, two hotels and a shop selling Blue Lagoon products.

The steamy Blue Lagoon

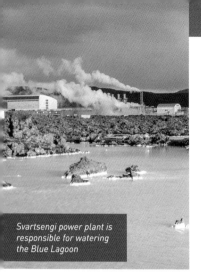

Svartsengi power plant is responsible for watering the Blue Lagoon

In spite of its evocative name, the lagoon is not a natural phenomenon but a fortuitous by-product of Iceland's geothermal energy usage. The nearby Svartsengi power plant pumps up superheated saltwater from 2km (1.25 miles) underground. This water is used to generate electricity and heat fresh water, after which it flows into the lagoon. Rich in silica, salt and other minerals, the run-off is great for your skin! The lagoon has Blue Flag certification for its water quality, and its nine million litres of saltwater are renewed every 40 hours.

Due to overwhelming visitor numbers, it is now obligatory to prebook online. Although you must turn up at the right time, you can then stay as long as you like. People spend an average of two hours bathing in the balmy waters. Bathing suits, towels and bath robes can be rented at the reception.

Most hotels have details of Blue Lagoon tours, but it is cheap and very easy to get there by public transport. There are hourly buses (7am to 8pm) from the BSÍ bus station in Reykjavík to the lagoon, returning at quarter-past the hour (11.15am to 11.15pm). Some buses to/from the international airport also call at the lagoon (which has luggage-storage facilities for suitcases) – see www.re.is/blue-lagoon-schedule for details.

THE GOLDEN CIRCLE

The Golden Circle, a 200km (125-mile) round trip from Reykjavík, takes in some key historical and geological attractions, including the site of the country's first parliament, an impressive geyser field and one of Iceland's most dramatic

⊘ THE PARLIAMENT AT ÞINGVELLIR

Þingvellir may feel as if it's in the middle of nowhere, but 1,000 years ago it was the focal point of the country. For two weeks every summer, Icelanders flooded into the valley to take part in or just watch the proceedings of the Alþingi (parliament). The position was perfect, with plenty of grazing land for horses, good tracks from the more populated parts of Iceland and a lake teeming with fish to feed the multitudes. Trading and socialising went on continuously while the leaders got on with the serious work of running the country. It was the job of the 36 chieftains from the various regions to agree on new laws, under the supervision of the 'law speaker'. A Law Council, made up of four regional courts and a supreme court, dealt with infringements and disputes. Huge fines could be imposed, and for the most serious crimes the offenders were outlawed from the country, but the system relied on the population to accept its authority voluntarily. It didn't have the power to stop open warfare from breaking out when disputes couldn't be resolved peacefully. From the mid-16th century the courts gained more power, and public executions took place. Men were beheaded, and women convicted of witchcraft or sexual offences were drowned in the river. Alþingi's last meeting was held here in 1798. After that a national court and parliament was established in Reykjavík.

Þingvellir National Park

waterfalls. The whole area is rich with medieval history and provides the setting for many of the sagas. There are numerous tours from Reykjavík, taking about eight hours, and including stops at gift shops and eating places along the way. With careful planning, the trip can be done by public transport. If you are hiring a car, the route is well signposted and parking is good.

Þingvellir

The nearest of the Golden Circle sights to the capital is **Þingvellir National Park** ㊾, the spiritual and historical heartland of Iceland, and a Unesco World Heritage Site thanks to its marvellous natural setting and unique glimpse of medieval Norse culture. Þingvellir (parliament plains) was the site of Iceland's original Alþingi (parliament), established in 930, which laid the ground for a common culture and national identity. The last þing was held here in 1798, after which the parliament moved to Reykjavík.

There are few actual monuments or buildings to be seen, so you have to use your imagination to picture the events of the past, but the national park, a sunken rift valley between the plate boundaries, is a beautiful spot. On the horizon in every direction lie low volcanic mountains, snow-capped for much of the year. Wildflowers cover the plain in summer, and in autumn it turns sumptuous shades of red.

Above the rift, at the Almannagjá viewing point, a **visitor centre** (daily 9am–6.30pm) contains interactive displays about the park. From the viewing point, you can see the rift valley clearly, where the North American and European continental plates are slowly moving apart, widening Iceland by 1.5cm (0.6ins) a year. From here, you can walk down a path to the **Alþingi site** itself: a flagpole marks the Lögberg ('Law Rock'), from where the leader of the parliament, the law speaker, made his proclamations. Further northeast along the rift is the Drekkingarhylur, or 'drowning pool', where adulterous women met a ghastly fate; a little further again the pretty Öxaráfoss waterfall tumbles into the valley.

On the eastern bank of the river is the glistening white Þingvallabær farmhouse and the red-roofed **Þingvallakirkja** (mid-May–Aug daily 9am–5pm), which dates from 1859. At the back is a site reserved for the burial of notable Icelanders, although only two tombs have been allowed so far, both of patriotic poets. Just northeast of the church is **Peningagjá**, a deep water-filled rift that is now a wishing well full of coins from all over the world.

Around 3km (1.8 miles) northeast of the church, near the Leirar campsite, is the **main information centre** (www.thing vellir.is; daily 9am–6pm, June–Aug until 10pm), with a café

A film-maker's dream

Unearthly scenery – and generous subsidies for film-makers – mean Iceland has starred in numerous films and TV programmes, often as an alien planet (*Prometheus*; *Star Wars: Rogue One*; *Star Trek: Into Darkness*) or a fantasy realm (*Game of Thrones*; *Thor: The Dark World*).

and shop selling maps and books about the area.

Dive.is (tel: 578 6200; www.dive.is; prebooking necessary) offers snorkelling and scuba diving (drysuit certificate required) in the **Silfra rift** that cuts into Þingvallavatn lake.

Geysir

The next Golden Circle target is 25km (16 miles) away at **Geysir ⑩**, which gave its name to all such water spouts around the world. Sadly, the Great Geysir, which started erupting in the 13th century and once reached heights of up to 80 metres (260ft), has been dormant for decades. As far back as the 1930s, the English poet W.H. Auden noted that Icelanders were pouring in soap – a sort of Viagra for geysers – to encourage eruptions. An earthquake in 2000 briefly woke the Great Geysir up: it erupted for two days straight, reaching 122 metres (400ft) in height, then settled into slumber once again.

Luckily, the Great Geysir's ever-reliable neighbour, Strokkur ('the churn'), bursts upwards every 10 minutes or so to a height of up to 30 metres (100ft). Stand up-wind of its bulging blue eye to avoid the scalding water.

The whole area is geothermically active, with the devilish smell of sulphur (similar to the smell of a rotten egg) wafting gently in the wind. Walking trails are marked out among steaming vents, turquoise pools and glistening, multicoloured mud formations. Make sure you stick to paths, and resist the temptation to step over ropes or stick your fingers in any pools: every year people's holidays are wrecked by severe burns – don't let it happen to you.

Gullfoss

The third Golden Circle treat is just 9km (6 miles) from Geysir. **Gullfoss** ③ (Golden Falls; http://gullfoss.is) is another example of nature at its most forceful, a deafening double waterfall where the River Hvítá drops 32 metres (105ft) before thundering away down a 2km (1.2-mile) -long canyon. A path from the parking area leads down to the waterfall's northern face, allowing you to feel the thunder at close range. Wear something waterproof, as the clouds of spray that create photogenic rainbows on sunny days will douse you from head to foot.

By the café, a small exhibition space remembers Sigríður Tómasdóttir, a local farmer's daughter who in the 1920s protested against plans to build a dam above Gullfoss. The government ended up purchasing the falls and making them a national monument.

Other Golden Circle stops

Depending on the tour company, or your own independent schedule,

Stunning winter landscape at Gullfoss

Skálholt's 1960s cathedral

you might also stop at the following places on the Golden Circle route:

Laugarvatn. On the shore of a lake of the same name, Laugarvatn is a popular holiday spot for Icelanders, about 30km (19 miles) from Þingvellir and en route to Geysir/Gullfoss. The small town is built on a geothermal spring: you can bathe in the mineral-rich waters at **Laugarvatn Fontana Geothermal Baths** (Hverbraut 1; tel: 486 1400; www.fontana.is; daily early June–Aug 10am–11pm, rest of the year 11am–10pm; charge), which has warm pools, hot pots and three steam rooms. Their café also sells lava bread baked in the hot black sand. Two hundred metres/yds away, the historical hot spring **Vígðalaug** was used as an all-weather baptism spot by Iceland's first Christians.

Flúðir. About 30km (19 miles) south of Gullfoss, Flúðir is another very active geothermal area, famous for its mushroom-growing. In this village is the **Secret Lagoon** (tel: 555 3351; www.secretlagoon.is; daily May–Sept 10am–10pm, Oct–Apr 11am–8pm – ticket sales stop 50 minutes before closing; charge), a lovely natural geothermal pool with bubbling hot springs nearby.

Skálholt. Skálholt was the site of one of Iceland's two all-powerful bishoprics from 1056 until the late 18th century. Notoriously, during the Reformation, the last Catholic bishop,

Jón Arason, and his two sons were beheaded here in 1550. Looking at the modern 1960s **cathedral** (daily 9am–7pm), peaceful in the quiet green farmland, it's hard to imagine such bloodshed and turmoil. Fine stained-glass windows, the work of artist Gerður Helgadóttir, bathe the interior in rippling colour. In the basement is a small exhibition (charge) where you can see the 13th-century sarcophagus of one of the early bishops, Páll Jónsson. When the sarcophagus was unearthed, Páll's skeleton was found to be clutching a crozier beautifully carved from a walrus tusk, now on display in the National Museum in Reykjavík (see page 42). Outside is **Þorláksbúð**, a reconstruction of a 16th-century turf-roofed building. Skálholt hosts the country's oldest summer music festival (www.sumartonleikar.is), a five-week series of Baroque and contemporary concerts.

THE SOUTH COAST

Iceland's beautiful south coast is a long green strip, dotted with tiny farms and bordered by waterfalls and glacier tongues on one side, and the crashing waves of the Atlantic on the other. The 'standard' south-coast bus tour runs as far as the village of Vík, a 360km (223-mile) round trip from Reykjavík, taking around 10 hours. Stops usually include Sólheimajökull glacier, Reynisfjara black-sand beach and the waterfalls Skógafoss and Seljalandsfoss. Some tour companies offer longer day trips (16 hours) that head further east to Skaftafell nature reserve and Jökulsárlón glacier lagoon (745km/463-mile round trip). Public buses along the south coast are not frequent enough to hop on and off at each sight in a day; but you could do it by public transport over several days; or hire a car, giving you more flexibility and freedom.

The mountains along Iceland's south coast are tantalisingly close, but require specialised transport. In high summer, some public (mountain) buses run into the interior, for example to Þórsmörk nature reserve, but they are more suited to people making multi-day hikes, rather than day-trippers.

Tour to Vík

Tour buses head east from Reykjavík on the Ring Road (Route 1), carrying you over the high heath and smoking earth of Hellisheiði before descending to the southwestern plain. They pass through **Hveragerði** ⑤, whose geothermal greenhouses provide the country with cut flowers, tomatoes and exotic bananas and papayas, and the large service town Selfoss, before crossing the Þjórsá, Iceland's longest river, into horse country. Over the next 100km (60 miles), Hella (pop. 800) and Hvolsvöllur (pop. 900) are the biggest settlements you'll see.

You can generally spot the clouds of spray from **Seljalandsfoss** ⑤ waterfall long before you reach it. The water topples 60 metres over a hollowed-out cliff, meaning you can walk right behind the falls. The river originates from Eyjafjallajökull glacier, famous for the subglacial volcano that erupted in 2010, covering everything for miles around in thick grey ash and resulting in the largest air-traffic shut-down since World War II.

Ten kilometres (6 miles) east is the tiny village of **Skógar** ⑤. **Skógafoss**, another stunner of a waterfall, crashes down from nearby cliffs and is extraordinarily photogenic. Legend tells that the first settler at Skógar hid his treasure beneath the falls. Skógar is also home to a fantastic **folk museum** (www.skogasafn.is; daily June–Aug 9am–6pm, Sept–May 10am–5pm; charge): some bus tours include entry to its 15,000-piece collection, which includes a reconstructed church, a school and a driftwood house. Just to the east, most tours stop at

Sólheimajökull , where you can walk to the foot of the glacier and stare into the icy waters of the lagoon.

Reynisfjara beach, with black sand and basalt columns, makes another photogenic stop. Keep well away from the water – freak waves have killed several people over the years. The last port of call is the coastal town of **Vík** 56, set beside a dramatic stretch of coastline: here the North Atlantic swell smashes down onto a long beach of black sand and three distinctive stone steeples, known as Reynisdrangar, rise out of the sea. Legend has it that they are trolls who were turned to stone as they pulled their three-masted ship ashore. Far more monstrous are the aggressive Arctic terns – Vík contains one of Iceland's largest breeding colonies. Bus tours stop for lunch at the small service station before heading back to

Mighty Skógafoss

Reykjavík (bring your own packed lunch to make more time for sight-seeing).

Onwards to Jökulsárlón

Although Vík is the furthest that most south-coast bus tours will bring you, some longer 16-hour trips continue as far as the glacial lagoon Jökulsárlón. The road east is both bewitching and ghastly, crossing lava plateaus and plains of smoke-coloured sand, threaded with glittering grey streams. Everything you see has been brutalised by immense natural forces – gouged by ice, scorched by molten rock, inundated by glacial floods.

In the middle of this wasteland is the hamlet of **Kirkjubæjarklaustur ⑰**, first settled by Irish monks, and then the site of a medieval Benedictine convent. Prayers certainly paid off in Klaustur during the devastating 1783 Laki eruptions. The local pastor delivered the ultimate fire-and-brimstone sermon to his flock, as a flow of lava headed inexorably towards the hamlet. When the sermon ended, the congregation stumbled outside to find that the lava had miraculously changed course, sparing the church and people.

Further east, you enter the domain of massive Vatnajökull, Europe's largest icecap at almost 150km (90 miles) across. It dominates the southeastern corner of Iceland, sending its glaciers flowing down the mountains into a beautiful desolation of sand and water. **Vatnajökull National Park**, created to protect the icecap, covers 13 percent of Iceland's total area. **Skaftafell ⑱** is the most popular part of the park, with two Saga Age farms, rugged mountains, waterfalls and three glaciers. Tour buses stop at Skaftafell visitor centre.

Continuing east, the next major point of interest is the extraordinary glacier river lagoon at **Jökulsárlón ⑲**. Great slabs of ice that have broken off Breiðamerkurjökull glacier float serenely in the water, some as big as houses. The lake only formed in the 20th century, but climate change has seen the glacier melt so quickly that Jökulsárlón is now the deepest lake in Iceland. Some bus tours include a boat trip (http://icelagoon.is; 40 per day July–Aug, fewer at other times; charge), allowing you to float among the

The icy world of Skaftafell

glistening ice formations, although you can see the icebergs just as well from the shore.

SNÆFELLSNES

The drive immediately north of Reykjavík is, to start with, less rewarding than heading southeast. However, if you make it as far as the **Snæfellsnes peninsula ⑥**, you will experience one of the most scenic parts of the country – almost an Iceland in miniature. Several tour-bus companies run 12- to 13-hour day trips to Snæfellsnes, allowing you to admire its spectacular mountainsides, waterfalls, black-sand beaches and ancient fishing villages. You could also hire a car and make your own way there.

After the well-maintained roads of Reykjavík and the Ring Road north, branching out onto the Snæfellsnes peninsula is quite an experience. Very quickly you will get the sense of being off the beaten track: the roads here can be windy and bumpy. The major bus tours generally head along the southern edge of the peninsula, stopping first at **Ytri-Tunga** beach, one of the most reliable places in Iceland to see seals, especially in summer, followed by a photostop at beautiful **Bjarnarfoss** waterfall. Some people see a *fjallkona* (Lady of the Mountain) inside the falls, with a veil of water droplets falling around her shoulders.

Tours then approach **Snæfellsjökull National Park**, bounded by the sea. At its heart is enigmatic **Snæfellsjökull**, a slumbering glacier-crowned volcano 1,445 metres (4,740ft) high. The glacier was made famous by Jules Verne as the entry point for his *Journey to the Centre of the Earth*, and also plays a role in *Under the Glacier* by Nobel Prize-winning Icelandic novelist Halldór Laxness.

At its foot on the south shore lie two tiny settlements, Hellnar and Arnastapi. Bus tours generally stop at the seaside café in **Hellnar** for lunch, before dropping you off in **Arnastapi** for a walk along the cliffs. The 2.5km (1.5-mile) stretch of coast between the two places is a lovely nature reserve, packed with birdlife and fascinating basalt formations, ravines and grottoes. The huge stony statue guarding Arnarstapi is Bárður Snæfellsás – half man, half troll – who was one of the original Norwegian settlers in this region. After a family dispute, Bárður pushed both his nephews off a cliff, gave away all his possessions and disappeared into the glacier. Since then, his spirit is said to protect the area, and is called on in times of need.

More wild and twisted lava formations are on offer on the short walk down to **Djúpalónssandur**, a dramatic black-sand beach, and **Dritvík**, a natural harbour circled by high lava walls. Standing out rusted red against the sand are the protected remains of a shipwreck, all that is left of a British trawler that sank in 1948 with the loss of 14 lives. Back on the main road, tours generally stop at Saxhóll crater: a set of stairs runs to the top, from where there are great views of the sea and mountains.

Around the peninsula is **Ólafsvík**, a peaceful but highly productive little fishing town. Its distinctive church (1967) was built to resemble a ship when viewed north-to-south, and a dried codfish from above. Independent visitors might consider a whale-watching trip (Láki Tours; tel: 546 6808; www. lakitours.com; Apr–Oct) – this is the best place in Iceland to see killer whales and sperm whales.

Further east, Grundarfjörður's perfectly symmetrical mountain **Kirkjufell** is the most-photographed in Iceland

Photogenic Kirkjufell

– even more so since it starred as 'mountain shaped like an arrowhead' in *Game of Thrones*.

From here, tour buses head home to Reykjavík. If you are travelling independently, you might consider staying overnight in attractive **Stykkishólmur**, full of brightly painted wooden houses. **Norwegian House** (Norska Húsið; www.norskahusid.is; May–Aug daily 11am–6pm, Sept–Apr Tue–Thu 2pm–5pm; charge) is decorated with period furniture and antiques, as it looked when William Morris stayed there in 1871. Also worth investigating is the **Library of Water** (Vatnasafn; https://www.facebook.com/vatnasafn/; June–Aug daily 10am–5pm, Sept–May Tue–Sat 11am–5pm; charge), formerly a library and now a contemplative installation by American artist Roni Horn; and the **Volcano Museum** (Eldfjallasafn; www.eldfjallasafn.is; May–Sept daily 10am–5pm; Oct–Apr Tue–Sat 11am–5pm; charge), set up by a local volcanologist to give visitors an insight into Iceland's explosive character. Daily summer **boat tours** (www.seatours.is) sail around some of Breiðafjörður's 2,700 tiny islands from the pretty little harbour, catching crabs, scallops and starfish for passengers to snack on.

DAY TRIPS BY PLANE

It might sound like a wild idea, but thanks to efficient domestic flights, it's also possible to fly off for the day. Air Iceland Connect has five reasonably priced daily flights from the domestic airport in Reykjavík to Akureyri in the north, taking a mere 45 minutes. Catching the first would get you to Akureyri in time for breakfast, with 12 hours to explore the town before catching the last flight back. Similarly, Eagle Air (Flugfélagið Ernir) has summer flights (weather permitting) from Reykjavík domestic airport southeast to the island of Heimaey in the Vestmannaeyjar chain, daily except Saturday. This gives you seven or eight hours to explore its volcanic curiosities.

AKUREYRI

Akureyri , the capital of the north, is a thriving metropolis by Icelandic standards. It is the country's second 'city', although its 18,200-strong population makes it more of a provincial town. It is an attractive place, however, with snowcapped granite mountains and a sheltering fjord that protect it from Arctic winds. Despite being only 100km (60 miles) from the Arctic Circle, it enjoys some of the country's warmest weather, bringing the flowers, café tables and people out into the pedestrianised streets in summer.

Summer in Akureyri

Akureyri stretches in a long, narrow ribbon by the water; however its shopping centre and old town are compact enough to explore on foot. You will need to walk (3km/2 miles) or take a taxi (around ISK1,500–2,000) into town from the airport, which is located south of the centre.

Port and town centre

Akureyri's fjordside port usually contains picturesque trawlers or an impressive cruise ship. Several companies offer three-hour **whale-watching trips** – humpbacks and minkes are often seen in Eyjafjörður, which is Iceland's longest, deepest fjord. Hof Culture Centre contains the town's **tourist office** (Strandgata 12; tel: 450 1050; www.visitakureyri. is; June–mid-Sept daily 8am–6.30pm, May and late Sept Mon–Fri 8am–5pm, Sat–Sun 8am–4pm, Oct–Apr Mon–Fri 8am–4pm), where you can pick up information or book trips. Also by the port, **Into the Arctic** (Norðurslóð; Strandgata 53; https://nordurslod.is; Mon–Fri 11am–6pm, Sat & Sun 11am–5pm; charge) is a fascinating exhibition that follows two early-20th-century Icelandic explorers on expeditions to Greenland and Arctic Canada, looking at boats, equipment, wildlife and Inuit culture, as well as offering visitors a virtual dogsled ride.

Follow Strandgata to get to the town centre. The main shopping street is partly pedestrianised **Hafnarstræti**, where all the hustle and bustle (such as it is) takes place – take time to explore the shops, stop for coffee or pick up some souvenirs. At the crossroad with Kaupvangsstræti, your eyes will inevitably be drawn upwards to the twin steeples of **Akureyrarkirkja**, especially dramatic when spotlit against the night sky. This eye-catching building was designed by architect Guðjón Samúelsson, who also designed Hallsgrímskirkja in Reykjavík. It's worth climbing the 102 steps for sparkling fjord views. Inside the church, the middle stained-glass window in the choir comes from the UK's original Coventry cathedral. It was removed at the start of World War II, before the cathedral was destroyed by bombs, and rescued from a London antiques shop. Other notable features are the huge organ with 3,300 pipes, and the votive ship hanging from the ceiling. Back at the bottom of the steps, **Akureyri Art Museum** (Kaupvangsstræti 8; late

May–Sept daily 10am–5pm, Oct–late May Tue–Sun noon–5pm; charge) was expanded in 2018 as a 25th birthday present: old and new galleries celebrate the visual arts with ever-changing contemporary exhibitions.

Up the hill, the town **swimming pool** (Þingvallastræti 2; Mon–Fri 6.45am–9pm, Sat & Sun 9am–6.30pm; charge) is one of the best in the country, with two outdoor

Colourful blooms at Akureyri Botanical Garden

pools, an indoor pool, two waterslides, hot tubs, a steam room and sauna. In summer, there are extra distractions for children, including mini-golf and electric cars.

South of the centre

Akureyri takes righteous pride in its pretty **Botanical Garden** (Lystigarðurinn; Eyrarlandsvegur; June–Sept Mon–Fri 8am–10pm, Sat and Sun 9am–10pm; free), a blessing of the milder weather in this part of Iceland. There are 6,600 different plants from southern Europe, Africa, South America and Australasia, as well as examples of just about every variety that grows in Iceland. It's a lovely place for a summer stroll and coffee in the garden café.

Heading south down Hafnarstræti eventually brings you to Aðalstræti, a leafy street containing charming stretches of 19th-century buildings, including **Nonni's**

House (Nonnahús; www.nonni.is; June–Aug daily 10am–5pm, Sept–Oct Thu–Sun 10am–5pm; charge). This tiny, black, wooden construction was the home of Reverend Jón Sveinsson, nicknamed Nonni, whose children's books were translated into 40 languages and are still well-loved in Iceland and continental Europe. Nearby, the permanent exhibition at **Akureyri Municipal Museum** (Minjasafnið á Akureyri; Aðalstræti 58; www.minjasafnid.is; daily June–Sept 10am–5pm, Oct–May 1–4pm; charge) examines the life and times of the town's 19th-century inhabitants.

Two machine-focused museums lie between Aðalstræti and the airport: the **Industry Museum** (Iðnaðarsafnið; Eyjafjarðarbraut vestri; www.idnadarsafnid.is; June–mid-Sept daily 10am–5pm, mid-Sept–May Sat 2–4pm; charge)

Aviation Museum, Akureyri

details Akureyri's 20th-century industrial heritage; and the **Motorcycle Museum of Iceland** (Mótorhjólasafn Íslands; Krókeyri 2; www.motorhjolasafn.is; mid-May–Aug daily 11am–5pm, Sept–mid-May Sat 3–7pm; charge) covers the 100-year-old history of Icelandic motorbikes.

Back at the airport, a hangar-full of gliders and aircraft tell the story of flight in Iceland at the **Aviation Museum** (Flugsafn Íslands; www.flugsafn.is; mid-May–Sept daily 11am–5pm; charge).

HEIMAEY

The 16 tiny islands of the Vestmannaeyjar (Westman Islands) rise black and rugged from the cold sea, combining seductive isolation with raw natural beauty. The largest of the archipelago, and the only island that is inhabited, is friendly **Heimaey** ❷. It has a fascinating history, explored in several interesting museums, and blustery clifftop walks that will blow your socks off. The Vestmannaeyjar lie about 10km (6 miles) off the south coast of Iceland. Ferries leave from Landeyjarhöfn, southeast of the capital; or take the plane from Reykjavík domestic airport to visit on a day trip. However, do check the weather forecast before flying. It is not uncommon for clouds and rain to descend by mid-afternoon, closing off the airport.

In contrast to its harsh surroundings, Heimaey is one of the friendliest places in Iceland, its sense of community forged by remoteness and fickle nature. The town's precarious position on top of a volcano was brought into sharp focus on 23 January 1973, when a mile-long fissure cracked open without warning, and a wall of molten lava poured towards the town. By amazing good fortune, the entire fishing fleet was docked that night: the island was evacuated, with not one life lost. Over the next five months, 33 million tonnes of lava spewed from the fissure, burying houses and devastating the island. The eruption was over by July, and residents started returning to their altered home: the island was 2.2 sq km (0.84 sq miles) larger, and boasted a new mountain, Eldfell.

The drama of the eruption is explored at **Eldheimar** (http://eldheimar.is; May–Sept daily 11am–6pm, Oct–Apr Wed–Sun 1–5pm; charge), a small multimedia museum built around a house excavated from the lava flow – one of 370 homes that were buried. An excellent audioguide leads you around, and photos and interviews with eye-witnesses provide compelling first-hand accounts. The town's **Sagnheimar Folk Museum** (www.sagnheimar.is; May–Sept daily 10am–5pm, Oct–Apr Mon–Sat 1–4pm; charge), above the library, also has good coverage of the 1973 eruption, along with permanent exhibitions about the 17th-century pirate raids, when 242 islanders were captured and sold as slaves; the harrowing life of a fisherman at sea; and Heimaey's Þjóðhátíð Festival, one of Iceland's most famous cultural celebrations. A rough and cindery walking path leads to the top of 221-metre (725ft) -high **Eldfell**, allowing you to visit the cause of all the trouble. If you burrow a few inches down into the ground, you can feel the still-present volcanic heat.

Viking Tours (tel: 488 4884; www.vikingtours.is; mid-May–mid-Sept daily departures at 11am and 4pm; charge) set sail from Heimaey harbour, bouncing around the whole island on a 1.5-hour tour. Klettsvík bay, the craggy inlet to the left of the harbour mouth as you sail out, was being sectioned off at the time of writing to create a new home for two beluga whales released from an aquarium in Shanghai,

China. The **Sea Life Trust Beluga Whale Sanctuary**, which will include a visitor centre, is due to open in 2019. From the sea, you get great views of Heimaey's picturesque **Skansinn** area, where a replica stave church celebrates 1,000 years of Christianity; and of sun s bird cliffs, where hundreds of thousands of puffins, as well as guillemots, fulmars and 30 other types of seabird, come every year to nest and breed.

Back on dry land, naturalists might like to visit **Sæheimar Aquarium** (Heiðarvegur 12; http://saeheimar.is; May–Sept daily 10am–5pm, Apr & Oct Mon–Fri 2–3pm, Sat 1–4pm, Nov–Mar Sat 1–4pm; charge), where there is a small display of live Icelandic fish. The aquarium also acts as a bird rescue centre and sometimes has puffin chicks in season – they reek of raw fish, but it's still delightful to get so close to a puffling!

Heimaey's cute trademark puffins

Catching a gig at Harpa Norðurljós

WHAT TO DO

NIGHTLIFE

Dozens of small, bohemian café-bars dot Laugavegur, Bankastræti, Hverfisgata and Austurstræti. They keep a low profile among the shops, serving coffee and cakes and the odd evening beer until the weekend comes, at which point the gloves come off. The carousing starts after midnight, when shouted conversations, flowing booze, live music and dancing become the Friday- and Saturday-night norm. People pubcrawl from bar to bar in search of the hottest sounds and coolest vibe.

On weekend nights, bars often stay open until 5am (1am during the week) and only tend to charge entrance fees if there's live music. Although most pubs are casual, people do get dressed up to go to smarter bars, and more exclusive places will turn you away if you're wearing jeans or trainers. In summer, at closing time, everyone heads in a good-natured gang to Lækjartorg square to join the snaking queues at the hot-dog stalls.

As with most cities, clubs and pubs open and close in Reykjavík all the time, so it's worth asking around to find out where the newest and most fashionable places are. Two free publications, *The Reykjavík Grapevine* (fortnightly summer, monthly winter) and *What's On in Reykjavík* (monthly), are good starting points. Try **Gaukurinn** (Tryggvagata 22; http://gaukurinn.is), one of the biggest bars with live bands, karaoke and weekly English-language stand-up comedy; **Húrra** (Tryggvagata 22; http://hurra.is), in the same building as Gaukurinn, with a packed schedule of gigs; **Slippbarinn** (Mýrargata 2; www.slippbarinn.iccs), a favourite for cocktails; and **Austur** (Austurstræti 7), an upscale nightclub with one of the city's biggest dance floors.

For more cultural nights out, Reykjavík has its own ballet, opera, orchestra, theatre and dance groups. *What's On in Reykjavík* lists the latest performances. Harpa Concert Hall (Austurbakki 2; box office tel: 528 5050; www.harpa.is) is home to the Reykjavík Big Band, the Icelandic Opera and the internationally acclaimed Iceland Symphony Orchestra (https://en.sinfonia.is), who perform here from September to mid-June.

There are seven cinemas in the capital area. The most central is the four-screen **Bíó Paradís** (Hverfisgata 54; www.bioparadis.is), which shows newly released international and Icelandic films, as well as dusting off classics for your delectation. Foreign films are shown in their original language with Icelandic subtitles.

SHOPPING

Icelandic products are perfect for those who appreciate quality and smart design – if your credit card can take the strain. Most shops in Reykjavík are small, one-off boutiques, located within a relatively small area centred around Laugavegur. Good buys include books, unusual food, music, clothes, skincare products and beautifully made homeware.

Reykjavík's big bookshops, **Eymundsson** (Austurstræti 18) and **Mál og Menning** (Laugavegur 18) – open until 10pm daily – are delightful reflections of a literary nation. Both contain large English-language sections.

Cultural immersion

A brilliant way of meeting locals and learning about Icelandic culture is by taking part in a creative workshop – Creative Iceland (creativeiceland.is) offers everything from knitting to knife-making, photography to folk songs, and screen-printing to *skyr*-tasting.

Supermarkets sell salted liquorice (*salmiak*), a Scandinavian passion. The powerful schnapps *brennivín*, with its minimalist black label, makes a good gift for a liqueur connoisseur. **Omnom Chocolate Factory** (Hólmaslóð 4), at the Old Harbour, sells direct to the public from its factory shop.

Eymundsson is Iceland's oldest bookshop

Record-shop staff are usually happy to help you through the maze of homegrown music: shops include independent label **Smekkleysa** (Laugavegur 35; https://smekkleysa.net), **Reykjavík Record Shop** (Klapparstígur 35; www.facebook.com/reykjavikrecordshop), **12 Tónar** (Skólavörðustigur 15; www.12tonar.is) or Iceland's biggest record shop, **Lucky Records** (Rauðarárstígur 10; http://luckyrecords.is).

Traditional woollen gloves, scarves, hats and the distinctive *lopapeysa* (sweater) are made from one-of-a-kind Icelandic sheep's wool – beware of 'made in China' imposters. The **Handknitting Association of Iceland** (Handþrjónasamband Íslands; Skólavörðustigur 19; http://handknit.is) sells the real deal. Outdoor clothes companies **Cintamani** (http://cintamani.is), **Icewear** (www.icewear.is) and **66° North** (www.66north.com) make tough, warm, stylish clothes that keep the Icelandic weather out. Their clothes are for sale all over Iceland.

Piled woolies at the Handknitting Association of Iceland

The **Blue Lagoon** has a city-centre shop (Laugavegur 15; www.bluelagoon.com), selling skincare products that are especially good for people with dry skin or conditions such as psoriasis.

For Icelandic-designed homeware, try **Hrím** (Laugavegur 25; www.hrim.is); **Epal** (Laugavegur 70); and **Kirsuberjatréð** (Vesturgata 4; www.kirs.is), a collective of 11 female artists selling weird and wonderful goods: fishskin handbags, bowls made from radishes and music boxes woven from feathers.

There are two large shopping malls on the outskirts of the city: **Kringlan** (www.kringlan.is), with 180 shops/restaurants; and smaller **Smáralind** (www.smaralind.is; in Kópavogur), containing 90 businesses.

OUTDOOR ACTIVITIES

There can be few capitals in the world better located than Reykjavík for exploring the great outdoors. Hiking, horse riding, fishing, kayaking, swimming, birdwatching and whale-watching are all available right on the city's doorstep. A little further afield, but do-able on a day trip, are rafting, snorkelling/scuba-diving and glacier walks.

WHALE-WATCHING

Several companies operate whale-watching trips from Reykjavík's harbour, sailing out into Faxaflói bay up to six times per day between April and October. There's a 90 percent cetacean-spotting success rate in summer: you're most likely to spot minke whales, white-beaked dolphins and harbour porpoises, although humpbacks, fin whales and orcas are seen from time to time. Operators that abide by IceWhale's code of conduct for responsible whale-watching are: **Elding** (elding.is); **Special Tours** (www.specialtours.is); and **Whale Safari** (www.whalesafari.is).

PUFFIN TOURS AND BIRDWATCHING

Reykjavík is one of the few European capitals where geese and swans regularly overfly the main shopping street. The easiest place to watch birds is Tjörnin lake, beside the City Hall, where over 40 species congregate. These include ducks (eider, mallard,

⊘ TAX-FREE SHOPPING

Visitors can claim a VAT (Value Added Tax) refund if they have spent a minimum of ISK6,000 on goods in one transaction and will be taking their purchases home unused. Where you see the 'Tax-Free Shopping' sign, ask the shop assistant to sign a tax-free form, then when you are leaving Iceland take the unused purchases, the completed tax-free form, the original purchase receipts and your passport to an international refund point. In Keflavík Airport, the refund point is Arion Bank in the arrivals hall. Passengers must reclaim their VAT before checking in their luggage. For large purchases, where you are due to receive a refund of more than ISK5,000, you also need to get a stamp from the customs office.

gadwalls, scaup), geese, gulls and swans, plus a sizeable colony of Arctic tern towards the lake's southern reaches. For other city-centre birdwatching sites, see the 'Birdwatching in Reykjavík' brochure on the Fuglavernd (BirdLife Iceland; fuglavernd.is) website.

To see endearing little puffins, take a one-hour boat trip (run by the whale-watching companies listed above) from Reykjavík harbour. Depending on the tides, puffin tours sail around either Akurey or Lundey – between mid-May and mid-August these tiny islands are nesting sites for around 30,000 puffins.

HORSE RIDING

Icelandic horses are descended from the sturdy breed brought over by the Vikings, and are famous for their unique fifth gait, the smooth *tölt*. Farms and riding centres all over the country offer horse-riding treks lasting from one hour up to several weeks. Even in the Greater Reykjavík area there is a large choice, including **Viking Horses** (Almannadalsgata 19; vikinghorses.is), **Íslenski Hesturinn** (The Icelandic Horse; Surtlugata 3; www.islenskihesturinn.is) and **Sólhestar** (Surtlugata 19; www.solhestar.is), all clustered together near Heiðmörk conservation area, just southeast of the city centre; Íshestar

Icelandic horses are great for beginners

(www.ishestar.is) in Hafnarfjörður; and Laxnes Horse Farm (www.laxnes.is) in Mosfellsbær.

WALKING AND HIKING

Around 12km (7 miles) southeast of the city centre, Heiðmörk is the largest conservation area in Greater Reykjavík, and is threaded with walking and riding trails. Take a picnic and explore its woodlands, wetlands and volcanic features – the most well-known being the pseudocraters at Rauðhólar ('Red Hills'). Buses 5, 19 and 28 pass close by.

Hiking in Iceland generally requires previous experience, a high level of fitness and good hiking boots and waterproof clothing. The best months for hiking are June, July and August, but remember that Icelandic weather is capricious and prone to sudden changes even in summer. An excellent half-day hike leads up Mt Esja (909 metres/2982ft), about 10 kilometres (6 miles) northwest of the capital, with spectacular views of Reykjavík and the Reykjanes peninsula. Several trails ascend the mountain range, marked for different levels of difficulty. Most people stop at Steinn, a big rock 200 metres (656ft) below the summit, as the route becomes very steep and slippery after that. You can get to Esja by taking bus No. 15 to Háholt in Mosfellsbær, then bus No. 57 to Esjustofa café, at the foot of the mountain.

Around 30km (19 miles) east of Reykjavík is Hengill, an area of rich vegetation, hot springs, bubbling mud pools and extensive areas of lava and volcanic craters, criss-crossed by over 100km (62 miles) of hiking trails. It's important to stick to the clearly marked paths to avoid damaging the highly vulnerable Icelandic flora. You can reach Hengill on the Selfoss bus from the BSÍ terminal. The **Icelandic Mountain Guides** (www.mountainguides.is; June–Oct; charge) also offer a guided day trip from Reykjavík, with stops to explore a lava cave and bathe in a hot river.

GLACIER TOURS

Several Icelandic glaciers – alien places of meltwater, moulins and furry green 'mice' – are accessible in summer on a day trip from Reykjavík. The easiest to reach is Sólheimajokull, on the south coast (see page 75) – the **Icelandic Mountain Guides** (tel: 587 9999; www.mountainguides.is) and **Glacier Guides** (tel: 659 7000, 571 2100; www.glacierguides.is) both do city pick-ups. You need warm clothing and sturdy walking boots, but the guides provide you with ice axes, crampons and an explanation of glacier-walking techniques.

Hiking on Sólheimajökull glacier

RAFTING AND KAYAKING

Between mid-May and mid-September, you can raft the river Hvítá (which feeds Gullfoss waterfall on the Golden Circle route – see page 67). It's not the wildest water – the rapids are definitely 'beginner' level and suitable for anyone aged 11+ – but the scenery is wonderful, with Brúarhlöð canyon a particular highlight. **Arctic Adventures** (adventures.is) do pick-ups from Reykjavík.

The same company also takes small groups (minimum age 14) sea kayaking round the beautiful Geldinganes peninsula, a 10-minute drive northeast of Reykjavík centre. Such peace and quiet, so close to a capital city, is a true marvel – you may even see flocks of flittering puffins or the occasional curious seal.

SNORKELLING AND SCUBA DIVING

You need a dry-suit qualification to scuba dive in Iceland. **Dive.is** (tel: 578 6200; www.dive.is) offer the one-day PADI Dry Suit Course, plus daily diving and snorkelling tours to Silfra rift in Þingvellir National Park (see page 68), with pick-ups from Reykjavík.

FISHING

Salmon and trout fishing in Iceland have an international reputation: rivers must be booked months in advance. Permits are expensive, starting at around ISK40,000 per rod per day in peak season. The salmon season runs from 20 May to 30 September. Sea-run trout and char can be fished 1 April to 10 October; resident species can be fished year-round. For further information contact the Federation of Icelandic River Owners (tel: 563 0300; www.angling.is).

⊘ SWIM WITH THE TIDE

The swimming pool is to Icelanders what the pub is to Brits or the coffee shop is to New Yorkers. It's where people come to meet friends, relax and catch up on the latest gossip; in fact, it's even the place where MPs do much of their campaigning at election time! Although swimming pools across the city are friendly, relaxed places, there's strict etiquette governing their use. Since the level of chlorine in the water is very low, it's compulsory to shower thoroughly, with soap and without a swimming costume, before entering the water. Notices posted up in the changing rooms show clearly which parts of your body you need to wash before heading for the pool. Attendants are on the lookout and will send you back to the showers if you don't observe this basic requirement.

SWIMMING

More than just a sport in Iceland, swimming is a social activity for all the family. There are seven geothermally heated outdoor pools in the capital. The biggest is **Laugardalslaug** (Sundlaugavegur 30; tel: 411 5100; open Mon–Fri 6.30am–10pm, Sat & Sun 8am–10pm; charge), with a 50-metre (160ft) pool, hot pots, a Jacuzzi, steam room, sun lamps and children's pool with waterslide. Swimming costumes and towels can be hired for a small fee. For other city pools, see the Reykjavík City website (reykjavik.is/en/swimming-pools).

ACTIVITIES FOR CHILDREN

Reykjavíkers try to involve children in almost all their sporting and cultural activities. Swimming is particularly popular. The pool at Laugardalur (see above) has a huge 85-metre (280ft) waterslide and a children's pool. Nearby, the **Family Park and Reykjavík Zoo** has a good playground and lots of exciting animals.

Icelandic horses generally have very even temperaments and are good for young riders – see page 94.

Museums that will appeal to children include **Arbær Open-Air Museum** (see page 55), with farm animals and a playground with old-fashioned outdoor games; **Perlan – Wonders of Iceland** (see page 57), which has plenty of interactive exhibits; and the **Saga Museum** (see page 48), which will please bloodthirsty kids but might be too scary for the timid ones. Children interested in Vikings might also like the **Settlement Museum** (see page 38) and the **National Museum of Iceland** (see page 42), with activity areas where you can dress up as Vikings.

Teenagers may enjoy the bowling rink, **Keiluhöllin** (Öskjuhlíð; open Mon–Thu 2–10.30pm, Fri 2pm–1am, Sat 11am–1am, Sun 11am–10.30pm; charge), with a pizza restaurant attached.

CALENDAR OF EVENTS

6 January Twelfth Night. Marked with songs, bonfires and fireworks.

Mid-January–mid-February Þorrablót. At the half-way point of winter, this festival involves feasting on traditional delicacies such as lambs' heads and rams' testicles.

Early February Festival of Lights. Reykjavík's winter festival with arts and cultural events; winterlightsfestival.is.

1st Thursday after 18 April First day of summer. An optimistic celebration to herald the arrival of lighter days, marked with parades, sports events and gift-giving.

May/June Reykjavík Arts Festival. A two-week celebration of music, theatre, art and dance. Biennial – next held in 2020; www.listahatid.is.

1st Sunday in June Sjómannadagur (Festival of the Sea). A celebration of fishermen and the sea, taking place at the old harbour.

June 17 Independence Day. Large patriotic crowds gather in the city centre to celebrate the birth of the Republic of Iceland in 1944, with formal ceremonies in the morning and street theatre, parades and parties later in the day.

1st Monday in August (and preceding weekend) Verslunnarmannahelgi ('Shopkeepers' Weekend'). This bank holiday weekend sees city-dwellers head out to the countryside in droves for camping and music festivals.

Early August Reykjavík Pride. Annual six-day LGBTQ celebration; www.facebook.com/reykjavikpride.

Late August Menningarnótt. Reykjavík's Culture Night sees thousands of people strolling the streets, as museums, theatres and cultural institutions launch their annual programme of events. The night culminates in a firework display at the harbour.

Late August Reykjavík marathon. Held on the same day as Culture Night.

September/October Reykjavík International Film Festival. An 11-day extravaganza featuring both Icelandic and international films; www.riff.is

October/November Iceland Airwaves. A five-day tidal-wave of international indie/pop/rock; www.icelandairwaves.is.

31 December New Year's Eve. A satirical revue on television, followed by night-long outdoor parties with bonfires and fireworks.

EATING OUT

Icelandic food has undergone tremendous changes over the last 10 years, thanks to the influence of the 'New Nordic Kitchen' movement, with its focus on local, seasonal, sustainable produce. The restaurant scene has been hit by a great wave of energy, enthusiasm and experimentation, with new-found knowledge applied to traditional ingredients.

The country's top chefs take great pride in using Iceland's natural larder – fish, lamb, goose, reindeer, seaweed, moss, rhubarb – and reinventing and revitalising the lumpen, pickled, salted food of yesteryear. As a result, it's an exciting time to dine out in Reykjavík. Prices are high, but you are paying for excellent meals made with high-quality ingredients.

The shake-up has trickled down to Reykjavík's mid-range restaurants, which have also raised their game in the last decade, reinventing old classics for a modern palate. Many pubs and bistros prepare hearty, nourishing dishes inspired by 'grandmother's kitchen', which give you a chance to try Icelandic food without blowing up your bank account.

This small but outward-looking capital also has

Icelandic fine dining

plenty of international restaurants to try, lending Icelandic ingredients additional flavours from the Mediterranean to the Far East.

Most menus offer at least one vegetarian option, although vegan choices may be limited. Reykjavík restaurants are good at marking gluten-free dishes.

Food for thought

Ordering food and drink in Icelandic is not for the grammatically challenged. Anything you'd like must be in the accusative case since it's the object of your request. If in doubt, just remember *tvo bjóra—*perfect Icelandic for *two beers*!

MEAL TIMES IN REYKJAVÍK

In Reykjavík, many restaurants offer good-value fixed-price tourist menus or buffets in summer, with prices lower at lunch (often restricted to around noon–2.30pm). People tend to eat out relatively early in the evening, sitting down to dine between 6 and 7pm. Don't feel under any pressure to vacate your table one you've finished dinner – it's not common practice in Iceland to turf guests out once they've finished coffee to make way for the next sitting. Restaurants in the city tend to be open all day from about 11.30am until 10 or 11pm, so you don't have to be too organised about when you eat.

WHAT TO EAT

Fish and meat

The two staples of Icelandic cuisine are fish and lamb. Fish is cheap and plentiful, and every menu, from breakfast onwards, features it in some form or another. Fresh from the nearest fishing boat or glacial river, Icelandic fish – cod, haddock, halibut, herring, plaice, turbot, monkfish, salmon and Arctic char – is

Colourful cakes at Apótek restaurant

absolutely delicious. As for preserved fish, smoked salmon and gravadlax (sweet marinated salmon) are both of very high quality. A much-loved Icelandic snack, sold in supermarkets everywhere, is crunchy *harðfiskur* – wind-dried cod or haddock, torn into strips and eaten with butter. Shrimp, blue mussels and langoustine are the main types of shellfish you'll encounter.

The other Icelandic staple, lamb, may cost more, but the taste is exceptional. Sheep flocks graze wild in the highlands, eating herbs as well as grass, lending the meat a rich and gamey flavour. As with fish, lamb was traditionally smoked to produce *hangikjöt*, eaten hot or cold in thin slices. You'll see it served on rye bread in cafés, although it's traditionally a Christmas dinner treat, accompanied by béchamel sauce, peas, potatoes and pickled red cabbage.

A limited amount of game finds its way on to restaurant menus. In Iceland's eastern highlands, pink-footed geese and wild reindeer are hunted in late summer. Reindeer meat is similar to venison, and is served up as burgers in some restaurants, or as a Christmas pâté.

Dairy

Iceland's cows are fed on grass, rather than corn, and produce rich, tasty, nutrient-dense milk. Drink it straight, eat it as ice-cream or indulge in deliciously creamy *skyr*. Packed with calcium, high in protein and very low in fat, *skyr* is often described as yoghurt, but is technically a cheese. Every Icelander has his or her own favourite way of eating it: mixed with milk, sprinkled with sugar and fresh fruit, dolloped with jam or stirred into savoury dips and sauces.

Fruit and veg

Most fruit and vegetables are imported, and tend to be expensive and pathetic-looking after their travels. Reykjavík does have homegrown supplies of tomatoes and bananas, thanks to the huge geothermal greenhouses in southwestern towns like Flúðir and Hveragerði. Otherwise, the only vegetables that really thrive in the cold climate are potatoes, turnips, cabbages and rhubarb.

Hand-foraged seasonal items on New Nordic menus include seabirds' eggs in spring; bilberries, crowberries and wild strawberries in late summer; and wild mushrooms in early autumn.

Bread and cake

Visitors with a sweet tooth will love Iceland. Denmark had a profound influence in the early 20th century, and Iceland's coffee shops and bakeries are stuffed with mouthwatering Danish pastries (*vínarbrauð*). One of the most popular is the *snúður*, a spiral-shaped cinnamon roll, washed down with ice-cold chocolate milk.

Bread, often made with rye, accompanies every meal. Rye pancakes (*flatkaka*) go well with smoked salmon and other smorgasbord-type toppings. Something of a novelty, *hverabrauð* ('steam bread') is baked in underground ovens by the naturally hot earth.

Café Paris

WHAT TO DRINK

Coffee is the national drink of Iceland, consumed at all hours of the day and night. It's sometimes offered free in libraries, shops and supermarkets.

There are high taxes on alcohol, since – in common with other Nordic countries – the government tries to discourage consumption. Alcohol can only be bought in bars, restaurants and licensed government liquor stores (*vínbúð*). The main *vínbúð* outlet in Reykjavík is at Austurstræti 10a and has strictly limited opening times (Mon–Thu 11am–6pm, Fri 11am–7pm, Sat 11am–6pm). Very weak pilsner beer that is less than 2.2 percent can be bought in supermarkets.

Traditionally, drinking alcohol mid-week has not been part of Icelandic culture, although it is becoming more common to have a glass of wine or beer when dining out. A bottle of house wine over dinner will add around ISK5,000 to the bill. In Reykjavík, a growing craft-beer culture provides interest and variety. *Brennivín* ('burnt wine'), nicknamed 'Black Death', is a strong schnapps distilled from potatoes and flavoured with caraway seeds.

WHERE TO EAT

Reykjavík is such a small place that you can find a plethora of excellent restaurants and cafés in a very small central area. Most are located along Austurstræti, Hafnarstræti and the city-centre end of Laugavegur, and some of the surrounding streets. A cluster of superior seafood restaurants has popped up in the old fish warehouses on Geirsgata, by the harbourside. Grandi, approximately a kilometre northwest of the city centre, is an up-and-coming area where you might find interesting new bistros.

High-end and mid-range restaurants

To experience New Nordic cuisine, you'll need to head for the most upmarket of the city's restaurants. Fish and lamb feature heavily

⊙ TRADITIONAL ICELANDIC FOOD

For centuries Reykjavík was effectively cut off from the rest of the world. With food imports non-existent, and unable to grow much due to the harsh climate, Icelanders were more concerned with survival than the art of fine cuisine. People subsisted on a diet based almost entirely on fish, lamb and dairy products, with a few vegetables – cabbage, turnips, swedes and potatoes – being introduced in the 19th century. Food had to be preserved so it would last through the long winter months: meat and fish were smoked in sheep dung, salted, buried, wind-dried or pickled in whey.

Iceland's most infamous traditional foods reflect both the poverty and the resourcefulness of its earlier inhabitants, who could not allow any animal part to go to waste. Rotten shark (*hákarl*) is buried for three months until rubbery and rotten, chopped into small cubes, and swilled down with schnapps. Guts, blood and fat, sewn up in a sheep's stomach, pressed and pickled in whey, create haggis-like *slátur*. *Svið* are boiled and singed sheep's heads. A real delicacy, served on special occasions, is *súrsaðir hrútspungar* (pickled rams' testicles).

on menus, with more unusual sea urchins, seaweed, angelica and Icelandic moss arranged like works of art on your plate.

Seafood restaurants are generally excellent, showcasing the food that has sustained Iceland for centuries. Bistros do a great job of reinventing old dishes: try *kjötsúpa* (meat soup), *plokkfiskur* (fish stew) or even Arctic char smoked over sheep dung. Family-friendly restaurants offer burgers, pizza and pasta.

Cafés and bakeries

Reykjavík's cafés are cosy and multipurpose – many will serve you coffee and cake for elevenses, soup and ryebread at lunchtime, tapas for tea, then turn into a banging nightspot on a Friday night.

Bakeries are great for a cheap on-the-go lunch, selling sand-wiches and patisserie, and sometimes soups and salads.

Fast food

Iceland has roundly rejected McDonalds, sticking to its own ver-sions of fast food. The Icelandic hot dog, loaded with toppings, reigns supreme – Bæjarins Beztu, near Kolaportið flea market, is the capital's go-to late-night hot-dog stand.

⊙ ETHICAL EATING

Icelanders rarely eat whale meat (*hval*): in fact, the whaling in-dustry is largely sustained by tourists. The 'Meet Us, Don't Eat Us' campaign (http://icewhale.is) draws attention to the problem.

For centuries, Icelanders have happily munched cute little puffins, caught with giant fishing nets on the cliff tops. How-ever, over the last decade, climate change has severely affected breeding colonies, raising ethical questions about whether puf-fins should still be on the menu.

TO HELP YOU ORDER....

Could we/I have... **Gætum við/get ég fengið...**
menu **matseðill**
starters **forréttir**
main courses **aðalréttir**
desserts **eftirréttir**
snacks **smáréttir**
baked **bakað**
beer **bjór**
bread **brauð**

cheeses **ostar**
coffee **kaffi**
fried **steikt**
milk **mjólk**
rice **hrísgrjón**
smoked **reykt**
soup **súpa**
sugar **sykur**
water **vatn**
wine **vín**

...AND READ THE MENU

appelsínusafi orange juice
bleikja char
blómkál cauliflower
Fiskur (Fish)
franskar chips (French fries)
grænar baunir peas
gulrætur carrots
hangikjöt smoked lamb
humar lobster
kartöflur potatoes
kjúklingur chicken
lambakjöt lamb
laukur onion
lax salmon
lítið steikt rare
lúða halibut
lundi puffin
miðlungs steikt medium
nautakjöt beef

nautalundir beef fillet
nautasteik beef steak
rauðkál red cabbage
rauðspretta plaice
rófur turnips
rækja shrimp
salat salad
sandhverfa turbot
síld herring
silungur trout
skinka ham
skötuselur monkfish
steinbítur catfish
sveppir mushrooms
svínakjöt pork
te tea
vel steikt well done
ýsa haddock
þorskur cod

PLACES TO EAT

We have used the following symbols to give an idea of the price for a three-course evening meal for one, excluding wine.

$$$$	over ISK10,000
$$$	ISK5,000–10,000
$$	ISK2,500–5,000
$	under ISK2,500

REYKJAVÍK

Apótek $$$ *Austurstræti 16, tel: 551 0011,* http://apotekrestaurant. is. Apótek is a smart restaurant showcasing Icelandic specialities alongside Argentinean-style grilled beef (the chef is from Buenos Aires). Located in a stately building that once held Reykjavík's old apothecary, the building's history is acknowledged by 'pharmacists' who mix up great cocktails (painkillers, stimulants, tranquillisers and placebos!) to suit your mood.

Austur-Indíafélagið $$$ *Hverfisgata 56, tel: 552 1630,* www.austurindia. is. Indian spices and Icelandic ingredients turn out to be a perfect match: celebrate the happy marriage at this great little restaurant. Austur-Indíafélagið has some knockout one-of-a-kind dishes, such as tandooried Icelandic langoustines, and has been delighting diners for almost a quarter of a century.

Burro $$$ *Veltusund 1, tel: 552 7333,* www.burro.is. This cheerful tapas restaurant on the corner of Ingólfstorg square makes a refreshing change from Reykjavík's (admittedly excellent) sea of fish restaurants. It combines Latin and Icelandic influences to great effect, creating such mouthwatering novelties as Arctic char ceviche and duck tacos. Round off the night with cocktails at Pablo Discobar on the floor above.

Café Paris $$ *Austurstræti 14, tel: 551 1020,* www.cafeparis.is. Café Paris sits at the very heart of Reykjavík, overlooking Austurvöllur square and the Icelandic parliament. On a fine day, the outdoor tables provide people-watchers with a prime spot for a light lunch, a good cup of coffee and plenty of passersby.

Caruso $$$ *Austurstræti 22, tel: 562 7335,* www.caruso.is. Cosy Italian bistro in the centre of town, doing good pizzas and pasta dishes, fish and meat mains and healthy salads. Very welcoming with no pretensions. Caruso also has a newer site at the harbour (Ægisgarður 2), in a beautifully restored old saltfish warehouse, with a slightly shorter menu and wonderful sea views.

Dill $$$$ *Hverfisgata 12, tel: 552 1522,* www.dillrestaurant.is. A gourmet's delight, this elegant Scandinavian restaurant won Iceland's first Michelin star in 2017. It specialises in local organic ingredients, cooked in contemporary 'Nordic Kitchen' style. Five- or seven-course seasonal tasting menus contain dishes such as smoked haddock with blue mussels and reindeer with blueberry sauce.

Fiskfélagið (Fish Company) $$$$ *Vesturgata 2a, Grófartorg, tel: 552 5300,* www.fiskfelagid.is. This atmospheric fusion restaurant, under a little footbridge on Verturgata, gives traditional Icelandic ingredients an international makeover. If you have the stomach space, the seasonal 'Around Iceland' menu provides four courses of the freshest local food, prepared with great skill and imagination.

Gló $$ *Laugavegur 20b, tel: 553 1111,* www.glo.is. Canteen-style Gló, on the second floor, offers fresh, tasty daily dishes (one raw-food; one vegan; one meat), which make use of as many organic ingredients as possible. And if all the virtue gets too much, there's a tempting cake board...

Höfnin $$$ *Geirsgata 7c, tel: 511 2300,* www.hofnin.is. Based in one of the low-rise teal-coloured buildings with fabulous views of the small boat harbour, Höfnin is a cosy choice for seafood. As well as excellent shellfish soup, pan-fried fishballs and *plokkfiskur*, the atmosphere is friendly, and interesting fishing-related antiques add to the décor.

Horniŏ $$$ *Hafnarstræti 15, tel: 551 3340*, www.hornid.is. Although Reykjavík restaurants come and go at an alarming pace, Horniŏ has stood the test of time. It was the first Italian restaurant to open in Iceland (in 1979), and has been popular ever since. The atmosphere is relaxed and the pizzas, pasta and fish dishes are good.

Holt Restaurant $$$$ *Hótel Holt, Bergstaŏastræti 37, tel: 552 5700*, https://holt.is/restaurant. Holt is one of the capital's finest restaurants, an elegant, old-fashioned place serving top-notch cuisine. Creatively prepared fish, reindeer and lamb charm the tastebuds, while the museum-quality art collection provides a feast for the eyes. The hotel is tucked away in a residential district, midway between Tjörnin and Hallgrímskirkja.

Icelandic Street Food $ *Lækjargata 8*, www.icelandicstreetfood.com. Currently one of the most popular spots in town, Icelandic Street Food is fun, friendly and cheap, and fulfils its small menu to perfection. A fast-food place with a twist, it serves traditional Icelandic pancakes, fish stew and hearty lamb and shellfish soups. You'll have to fight for the few tiny tables.

Jómfrúin $$$ *Lækjargata 4, tel: 551 0100*, www.jomfruin.is. This lively place specialises in *smørrebrød* – Danish open sandwiches constructed with a rye-bread base, beautifully presented toppings, and washed down with schnapps. Ingredients are very traditional (herring, smoked eel, shrimp, caviar, liver pâté, bacon, roast beef, duck) – veggies will struggle! From June to August, there are Saturday afternoon jazz concerts.

Kaffivagninn $$ *Grandagarŏur 10, tel: 551 5932*, https://kaffivagninn.is. Reykjavík's oldest restaurant is a casual place near the harbour, and boasts fantastic views. The menu is short, but there is an excellent choice of Icelandic fish dishes. It's also a good place for breakfast (from 7.30am Mon–Fri) or Sunday brunch.

Kaffi Vínyl $$ *Hverfisgata 76, tel: 537 1332*. Iceland's first vegan café is laid back and lots of fun. As well as tasty, wholesome vegetarian and vegan food – like baked chickpeas, cinnamon pumpkin, roast aubergine and tofu – the live DJs and crackling vinyl collection lend a funky, hipstery vibe.

Kol Restaurant $$$$ *Skólavörðustígur 40, tel: 517 7474*, https://kolrestaurant.is. This small, cosy venue describes its offerings as 'feel good comfort food'. The fruits de mer, chargrilled salmon and tenderloin dishes are indeed hearty, but also presented in a beautifully artistic way. Ingredients show off the best of what has just been caught, harvested or foraged.

Lækjarbrekka $$$$ *Bankastræti 2, tel: 551 4430*, www.laekjarbrekka.is. In an atmospheric timber building dating from 1834, Lækjarbrekka is decorated with period furniture, chandeliers and heavy drapes, and is a classic choice for a special occasion. Gourmet set menus feature lobster, lamb and catch-of-the-day.

Matur og Drykkur $$$$ *Grandagarður 2, tel: 571 8877*, http://maturogdrykkur.is. In an old salt-fish factory at Grandi (same building as the Saga Museum), Matur og Drykkur is absolutely worth seeking out. Its menu delves deep into Icelandic culinary history, raising seaweed, cod's head and *kleina* to brand new heights. Evening dining is expensive, but there's a good-value set lunch.

Messinn $$$ *Lækjargata 6b, tel: 546 0095*, http://messinn.com. This roaringly successful fish-focused restaurant cooks up *plokkfiskur*, honey-glazed char and spicy redfish in rustic skillets, which are served directly to table. Messinn opened a second location (Messinn Granda, Grandagarður 8, tel: 562 1215) at Grandi harbour in 2017, where equally triumphant dishes are served as a fish buffet.

Ostabúðin $$$ *Skólavörðustígur 8, tel: 562 2772*, http://ostabudin.is. This gourmet delicatessen has a fantastic restaurant attached. A short, shrewd and well-executed menu tantalises the taste buds – the seafood soup and catch-of-the-day are some of the city's best. Table reservations are only taken up to 7.30pm, so be prepared to queue – it's worth the wait.

Skólabrú $$$$ *Pósthússtræti 17, tel: 511 1690*, http://skolabru.is. Dining – in this wooden family home from the early 20th century – is like stepping back in time. The elegant old-world ambience is complemented by beautifully presented food, with an emphasis on seafood, duck and game. Near Austurvöllur square, just behind the cathedral.

Snaps $$$ *Þórsgata 1, tel: 511 6677*, www.snaps.is. This bustling bistro-bar, serving French-Icelandic fusion food, is perfect if you like a bit of a buzz with your steak béarnaise. Clattering forks and merry chatter bounce around the inviting interior. Reservations are a must. Two streets south of Skólavörðustígur, near Hotel Óðinsvé.

OUTSIDE REYKJAVÍK (DAY TRIPS)

Akureyri

Rub 23 $$$ *Kaupvangsstræti 6, Akureyri, tel: 462 2223*, www.rub23. is/en. This polished fish restaurant is for those who like to play with their food. Choose your trout, lamb, chicken or beef; pick one of 11 marinades; then wait for the chef to cook your special combination – it's a little like watching a row of cherries come up on a fruit machine.

Blue Lagoon

Lava Restaurant $$$$ *Blue Lagoon, Grindavík, tel: 420 8800*, www. bluelagoon.com. Eat overlooking the world-famous thermal spa. The top-class restaurant cooks up contemporary dishes using local ingredients, such as blue mussels from Reykjanes, Arctic char flavoured with juniper, or creamy *skyr* with sorrel and rhubarb. Best enjoyed after, rather than before, a dip in the hot waters.

Golden Circle/South Coast

Ölverk Pizza & Brewery $$ *Breiðamörk 2, Hveragerði, tel: 483 3030*, www.olverk.is. Tours to the Golden Circle and South Coast pass through Hveragerði, where you'll find this excellent family-run pizzeria and brewery. Wood-fired pizzas are tasty and filling, and non-drivers can indulge in a range of craft beers which change with the seasons.

Heimaey (Vestmannaeyjar)

Gott $$$ *Barustigur 11, tel: 481 3060,* www.gott.is. The former head chef at Iceland's Hilton hotel now runs this fresh, modern restaurant, all in white with pops of bright colour. As well as fish of the day, there are juicy burgers, pulled pork, pastas and steak. Vegan and gluten-free dishes too.

A–Z TRAVEL TIPS

A SUMMARY OF PRACTICAL INFORMATION

A

ACCOMMODATION

The Vakinn star-rating system for accommodation in Iceland runs from five stars for the best facilities, down to one star for the most basic; however, the system is entirely voluntary and some places do not subscribe to it.

Reykjavík has a wide variety of hotels. Some are stylish, world-class places (with prices to match); some are boxy and impersonal; some are small and characterful. Sometimes it's hard to see what distinguishes the smaller 'hotels' from 'guesthouses' – both might be more intimate, family-run places, which offer cheaper rooms with shared bathrooms.

Iceland's four hotel chains are Íslandshotel (www.islandshotel.is), with 17 properties across Iceland including six in Reykjavík; Keahotels (www.keahotels.is), with nine hotels including six in Reykjavík; Icelandair Hotels (tel: 444 4000, www.icelandairhotels.com), with nine hotels including two in Reykjavík; and CenterHotels (www.centerhotels.com), which currently has six hotels in Reykjavík, with another two opening in 2019. International chains with a presence in the city are Hilton, Radisson Blu and (from 2019) Marriott. The best deals are available online.

Early bookings are strongly recommended for high season (mid-May to mid-September), when prices often double and rooms can be hard to come by. Outside these months, some hotels and guesthouses outside Reykjavík close for winter.

Elsewhere in the country, farms and guesthouses are the norm: Hey Iceland (tel: 570 2700, www.heyiceland.is) is a farmer-owned travel agency with over 170 farmhouses on its books. The free brochure *Áning* (available from tourist offices) lists hotels, guesthouses, summer houses, hostels and campsites countrywide. Inspired by Iceland (www.inspiredbyiceland. com) has an accommodation directory, searchable by type and location.

The two characteristics that almost all Icelandic accommodation options share are small rooms, especially when compared to US hotels and guesthouses, and thin walls and curtains – light sleepers should bring earplugs and an eye mask.

Over the last five years, many people have been using Air BnB (www.airbnb.com) to book rooms in Reykjavík; however, because it is such a small city, this has been causing terrible problems with the local rental market, and the government is now cracking down on unregistered homestays – before you book, make sure that your homestay displays a registration number (beginning 'HG-0000...'), or appears on the list of registered homestays here: www.syslumenn.is/skradar-heimagistingar.

AIRPORTS

Keflavík Airport (KEF; tel: 424 4000; www.isavia.is) is the international airport serving Reykjavík. The airport is 55km (35 miles) west of the city, on the Reykjanes peninsula. The Flybus (www.re.is/flybus; tel: 580 5400) and Airport Express (https://airportexpress.is; tel: 540 1313) leave the airport around 35 minutes after the arrival of every flight (including delayed ones), driving passengers to Reykjavík city centre. A return ticket costs ISK5,500 (ISK6,950 with hotel transfer) per person, and takes 45 minutes – buy tickets online or at the ticket machine or booth next to the airport exit. Buses stop at the long-distance BSÍ bus terminal in Reykjavík, from where there are minibus transfers on to most of the bigger hotels. The same journey by taxi is around ISK15,000 to ISK 20,000 for one to four people, and takes between half an hour and 45 minutes.

Reykjavík Airport (Reykjavíkurflugvöllur; RKV; tel: 424 4000; www.isavia.is) is the hub for domestic flights and services to Greenland and the Faroe Islands. The airport is around 2km (1.2 miles) south of the city centre. It's walkable; several city bus routes run fairly close by (see www.straeto.is); or a taxi costs from around ISK3,400.

B

BICYCLE RENTAL

You can hire bicycles from Reykjavík Bike Tours (Ægisgarður 7; tel: 694 8956; https://icelandbike.com; May–Sept daily 9am–5pm, phone at other times), near the whale-watching companies at the harbour; and from Reykjavik Campsite (see page 118), in Laugadalur valley.

BUDGETING FOR YOUR TRIP

Reykjavík's small population and high import costs make goods and services expensive.

Getting to Iceland. Icelandair (www.icelandair.co.uk/www.icelandair. com) is the main airline serving Iceland, operating from Europe and North America. You can find high-season Icelandair return fares to Reykjavík starting from £360 from the UK; and $470 from New York. Budget airline WOW Air (https://wowair.co.uk) has year-round departures from the UK, US and Canada, with high-season return fares costing around £180 (London Gatwick), $470 (New York) and C$700 (Toronto). EasyJet (www.easyjet.com) has year-round departures from the UK to Reykjavík, with high-season return fares costing around £200 from London. You may be able to hunt out better bargains by booking early and being flexible with dates. For more information on flights, see page 123.

Accommodation. In high season, a bed in a youth-hostel dorm costs from ISK4,800. A double room at a basic guesthouse with shared bathroom runs from ISK12,000; at a moderate hotel around ISK25,000; and at a deluxe hotel around ISK50,000.

Eating out. A main course for an evening meal in a budget restaurant costs from ISK3,000; at a moderate restaurant from ISK4,000; at an expensive restaurant from ISK5,000. A half-litre of beer at a bar or a glass of house wine at a restaurant costs around ISK1,200. A filter coffee is around ISK350, while a latte or cappuccino costs about ISK600.

Local transport. A single ticket for Reykjavík's city buses costs ISK460, and a one-day travelcard ISK1,700. The Reykjavík City Card (24/48/72 hours ISK3,800/5,400/6,500) gives you free bus travel within the capital area (plus free entry to swimming pools and certain museums, and a ferry trip to Viðey island).

Taxis are expensive: flagfall starts at ISK690, then rates rack up at ISK130 per minute plus ISK240 per kilometre (with the first two kilometres costing double).

Excursions. A whale-watching trip from Reykjavík harbour costs ISK11,000. An eight-hour tour to see the waterfalls and geysers on the Golden Circle is ISK8,000. Peak-time entry to the Blue Lagoon costs ISK9,990.

Money-saving tips. There's no getting around it – Reykjavík is expensive. Make sure you follow the locals' lead and buy your full alcohol allowance from the duty-free shop at Keflavík Airport when you first arrive in Iceland. Dining out bumps up bills considerably – renting an apartment with cooking facilities can help cut costs. The excellent two-hour City Walk Reykjavík (https://citywalk.is; booking recommended) sets off from Austurvöllur four or five times a day in summer, and costs as much as you think it's worth in tips. Reykjavík's fabulous geothermal swimming pools are a real bargain – admission is ISK980 (free with the Reykjavík City Card) – and the geothermal beach (see page 58) is free in summer. And of course, Iceland's glorious scenery is always free – admire the views from the sea-side Sculpture & Shore path; alternatively, explore Heiðmörk nature reserve or hike Mt Esja for the price of a local bus ticket (see page 51).

C

CAMPING

Reykjavík Campsite (Sundlaugarvegur 32; tel: 568 6944; www.reykja vikcampsite.is; camping ISK2,400 per person per night; reception open 24hrs/day mid-May–mid-Oct) is about 3km (2 miles) east of the city centre, in Laugadalur valley – bus No. 14 runs past it. It's a big, busy place, homing up to 900 people, with good facilities including a kitchen, free Wi-fi and free showers. The campsite is open year-round, but with limited facilities in winter (and whether you would want to camp in December is another matter!)

If you plan to visit the countryside with a tent, there are around 170 registered campsites in Iceland, usually open from June to August or mid-September – you can search for campsites on www.inspiredbyiceland.com.

Be aware that camping (in tents, caravans or campervans) outside designated campsites is now illegal without the landowner's written permission.

CAR HIRE (See also Driving)

Several major international rental companies are represented in Iceland, and there is an ever-growing number of local firms. You must be at least 20 years old to hire a car in Iceland. Car hire costs a minimum of ISK7,000 per day for a small city car (eg a Hyundai i10). Petrol is around ISK223 per litre, so it would cost ISK9,000 to fill the Hyundai tank. Insurance is compulsory and not always included in the quoted price, so check first.

Normal hire cars are not insured for the F-roads that cover the interior, thanks to boulder-strewn tracks and dangerous river crossings which require a four-wheel drive and lots of additional insurance.

The bigger companies are Hertz (tel: 522 4400; www.hertz.is), Europcar (tel: 461 6000; www.europcar.is), Avis (tel: 591 4000; www.avis.is) and Budget (tel: 562 6060; www.budget.is). For local operators, see the Visit Reykjavik website (https://visitreykjavik.is).

Note that queues for the car-hire outlets at Keflavík Airport can be long – it might be better to catch the Flybus into Reykjavík and hire a car from the city centre at a later time.

CLIMATE

Despite its proximity to the Arctic Circle, Reykjavík isn't that cold. It benefits from the Gulf Stream and is warmer than, for example, much of mainland Scandinavia. However, summers are generally cool, and the city is often wet and windy, with the weather changing dramatically from day to day and even hour to hour. Basically, it's sensible to be prepared for all eventualities. Unfortunately Iceland's weather generally approaches from the southwest, with the result that heavy rain clouds tend to empty their load on the Icelandic capital first before moving on elsewhere. The weather is drier and sunnier in the north and east, although no less windy. The temperature difference between summer and winter is remarkably small – in July and August, the average temperature is barely 14°C; whereas in December and January it's a respectable 2°C.

Average temperatures:

	J	F	M	A	M	J	J	A	S	O	N	D
°C min	-2	-2	1	1	4	7	9	8	6	3	0	-2
°C max	2	3	4	6	10	12	14	14	11	7	4	2

CLOTHING

Reykjavík's unpredictable weather means that layering is essential. Take a wind- and rainproof coat and a warm sweater, even in summer.

The dress code for pubs and bars is very relaxed – Icelanders are a tolerant bunch, and anything you're comfortable in is fine. You'll need slightly smarter attire for the more upmarket cocktail lounges and the city's few nightclubs – hoodies and trainers are definitely out. Dress well if you plan to visit the city's better restaurants, although even there, men, for example, wouldn't be expected to wear a tie.

A swimsuit is crucial so you can enjoy Reykjavík's many wonderful swimming pools and the Blue Lagoon.

CRIME AND SAFETY (See also Emergencies and Police)

Reykjavík is an extremely peaceful and law-abiding city. Violent crime is virtually non-existent. Petty theft occasionally occurs in swimming-pool changing rooms, bars and nightclubs, and there has been a small rise in pickpocketing in the last five years – use common sense, and keep an eye on your bag or wallet. Late-night drunken crowds can be noisy at weekends, but rarely threatening. If you are unfortunate enough to be a victim of crime, you can report it at Reykjavík's police station (Hverfisgata 113–115; tel: 444 1000).

The biggest risk to visitors is underestimating the terrain and the weather, which can be severe and change rapidly. If you go on any trips out of Reykjavík, stick to paths at waterfalls and high-temperature geothermal fields; absolutely do not dabble your fingers in boiling springs to test the temperature; don't climb on glaciers without a guide; and only drive on F-roads with a suitably insured 4WD and knowledge of the route. Hikers should be equipped with proper clothing and equipment, and let someone know where they are going. See https://safetravel.is for further information.

D

DISABLED TRAVELLERS

High kerbs, narrow doorways and small rooms can make wheelchair access difficult in Reykjavík's older buildings. Wheelchair access to Iceland's natural wonders is quite restricted, although the situation is improving. There are paved paths at Geysir, Gullfoss and Þingvellir National Park.

Þekkingarmiðstöð Sjálfsbjargar, an information centre for people with disabilities, is building up a database of accessible hotels, restaurants, tours and other services – see www.thekkingarmidstod.is/adgengi/accessible-tourism-in-iceland for details.

DRIVING

Although there are a staggering number of coach tours from Reykjavík, hiring a car does give you extra freedom and flexibility.

Road conditions. Ninety-nine percent of Route 1, the main Ring Road encircling the country, is surfaced. Once you turn off the main road, though, you may end up on narrow gravel or unmade roads, often full of potholes. Some roads are prone to flooding, and bridges are often single-lane. Sandstorms can be a hazard along the coast and in some parts of the interior. Sheep sometimes stand, lost in thought, in the middle of the highway; or a ewe might make a sudden dash across the road to be reunited with its lamb. Be prepared for journeys to take a lot longer than you might think from the distances involved, drive steadily and expect the unexpected.

In winter, strong winds, snow and black ice are common. Car-hire companies put winter tyres on their vehicles (and studded winter tyres may be available on request between November and mid-April), but unless you have experience of driving in adverse winter conditions, it might be better to leave the driving to a tour operator!

Rules and regulations. Icelanders drive on the right. Seat belts are compulsory in the front and back of a car, and headlights must be used at all times, day and night. The speed limit is generally 30kph (19mph) on residential streets, 50kph (30mph) on urban roads, 80kph (50mph) on out-of-town unmade roads and 90kph (55mph) on out-of-town paved roads. Speed cameras and speed traps are common, and speeding fines can be as much as ISK100,000.

Hands-free equipment is a legal requirement when using a mobile phone. Drink-driving, which is defined as 0.05 percent blood-alcohol content, is taken very seriously by the authorities. Offenders lose their licences and face heavy fines. Off-road driving is also illegal and dealt with very severely – Icelandic nature is extremely fragile, and moss torn up by tyres can take decades to recover. Offenders receive high fines and even prison sentences.

Fuel. In Reykjavik most petrol stations stay open until 11.30pm, and some are 24-hour. Around the Ring Road there are petrol stations every 50km (30 miles) or so, but if in doubt fill up before you move on. After-hours, some petrol stations have automated pumps. These don't take cash – you'll need a credit card with a four-digit PIN code, or you can purchase a pre-paid fuel card during opening hours for after-hours use.

Parking. Reykjavík's parking spots are divided into zones, with the most central P1 zone being the most expensive. On-street parking in P1 costs ISK320 per hour, while parking in central multi-storey car-parks costs between ISK80 and ISK200 per hour.

Help and information. For up-to-date information on road conditions, see www.road.is. You can also phone 1777 (8am–4pm summer, 6.30am–10pm winter) for information in English on how weather is affecting the roads. If your car breaks down, contact your car-hire company. If you are involved in a crash, tel: 112 for the emergency services. You can download the '112 Iceland' app, which helps first responders locate your vehicle in an emergency.

E

ELECTRICITY

The current in Reykjavík is 220 volts, 50 hz ac. Plugs are European round pin with two prongs.

EMBASSIES/CONSULATES

Australia: Australian Embassy in Copenhagen, Denmark, tel: (+45) 70 26 36 76, www.denmark.embassy.gov.au.

Canada: Túngata 14, 101 Reykjavík, tel: 575 6500, www.canada.is.

Ireland: Embassy of Ireland in Copenhagen, Denmark, tel: (+45) 35 47 32 00, www.dfa.ie/irish-embassy/denmark.

New Zealand: New Zealand Embassy in The Hague, Netherlands, tel: (+31) 70 346 9324, www.nzembassy.com/netherlands.

South Africa: South African Embassy in Oslo, Norway, tel (+47) 23 27 32 20, www.dirco.gov.za/oslo.

United Kingdom: Laufásvegur 31, 101 Reykjavík, tel: 550 5100, www.gov.uk/world/organisations/british-embassy-reykjavik.

United States: Laufásvegur 21, 101 Reykjavík, tel: 595 2200, https://is.usembassy.gov/embassy/reykjavik.

EMERGENCIES

To contact the police, ambulance or fire service, tel: 112.

G

GETTING THERE (See also Airports and Budgeting for your trip)

Apart from the weekly Smyril Line ferry (www.smyril-line.fo) from Denmark to eastern Iceland, the only way to get to Iceland is by air. International flights land at Keflavík Airport, 50km (30 miles) from Reykjavík.

Icelandair (www.icelandair.co.uk/www.icelandair.com) is the national Icelandic carrier, linking the country to Europe and North America. There are daily direct flights from the UK to Keflavík, from London Gatwick, London Heathrow, Glasgow and Manchester.

Icelandair flies direct to 21 cities in the US and Canada: Anchorage (summer only), Baltimore, Boston, Chicago, Dallas, Denver, Edmonton (summer only), Halifax (summer only), Kansas City (summer only), Minneapolis, Montreal (summer only), New York, Orlando (winter only), Philadelphia (summer only), Portland (summer only), San Francisco, Seattle, Tampa (winter only), Toronto, Vancouver and Washington. North American travellers flying with Icelandair across the Atlantic to European destinations can also make a free stopover in Iceland for up to seven nights.

Two budget airlines also fly to Iceland. WOW Air (https://wowair. co.uk), like Icelandair, connects European destinations with the US/ Canada via Iceland. UK flights depart year-round from London Gatwick, London Stansted and Edinburgh. The airline also flies from US and Canadian destinations, including Boston, Chicago, Cincinnati, Cleveland, Dallas, Detroit, Los Angeles, Montreal, New York, Pittsburgh, San Francisco, St Louis, Toronto and Washington.

EasyJet (www.easyjet.com) has year-round departures from London Gatwick, London Luton, London Stansted, Belfast, Bristol, Edinburgh and Manchester.

H

HEALTH AND MEDICAL CARE (see also Emergencies)

Thanks to its clean air and low pollution, Iceland is an extremely healthy place. Iceland's tap water is some of the purest in the world – buying bottled water is completely unnecessary. No vaccinations are required to visit Iceland, and the standard of medical care is very high.

Health insurance. An agreement exists between Iceland and countries within the EEA, including the UK, for limited health-insurance coverage of its residents. UK travellers should obtain the European Health Insurance Card (EHIC; www.ehic.org.uk) before leaving home. Be aware, however, that Brexit may affect reciprocal arrangements for UK citizens. Remember, also, that the EHIC isn't a substitute for travel insurance, which you need to buy separately. If you are planning to take part in any unusual or 'dangerous' sports, make sure that these are covered by your travel-insurance policy. You may have to pay first and reclaim the costs when you get home, so keep all bills and other documentation.

Pharmacies, hospitals and dentists. The Icelandic for pharmacy is *apótek*. Lyfja (Lágmúli 5, Reykjavík, tel: 533 2300) is open daily from 8am–midnight. There's also a Lyfja branch with shorter opening hours in the centre of Reykjavík, at Laugavegur 16 (tel: 552 4045; Mon–Fri 9am–6pm, Sat 11am–4pm).

For non-emergency medical treatment outside normal hours, the Læknavaktin Medical Centre helpline (tel: 1770) is open Mon–Fri 5pm–8am and 24 hours at weekends. They can provide telephone advice or send a doctor.

The 24-hour casualty department is at Landspítali University Hospital (Fossvogur, tel: 543 2000), or phone an ambulance directly on the emergency number 112.

For an emergency dentist, tel: 575 0505.

L

LANGUAGE

Iceland's centuries of isolation mean that Icelandic has stayed pretty uncontaminated since Settlement times – citizens can read the original Sagas with little trouble. Icelanders are extremely proud of their language and continue to protect it against foreign corruption. When new words are needed, the Icelandic Language Institute creates something appropriate from Old Norse roots – so a computer (*tölva*) fuses *tala* ('number') and *völva* ('prophetess'), while an astronaut (*geimfari*) combines *geimur* ('space') and *fari* ('traveller').

Nearly all Icelanders speak excellent English.

LGBTQ TRAVELLERS

Reykjavík has a relatively large and visible LGBTQ community, who have legal and social rights that are among the most progressive in the world. The country elected the world's first openly gay prime minister and passed a gender-neutral marriage bill in 2010. The annual six-day Reykjavík Pride celebration (https://hinsegindagar.is) is held every August, drawing over 100,000 participants and supporters.

The National Queer Organization/Samtökin '78 (4th Floor, Suðurgata 3, 101 Reykjavík, tel: 552 7878, e-mail: office@samtokin78.is, www.samtokin78.is) has an 'open-house night' between 8pm and 11pm on Thursdays.

More information about the gay scene in Iceland can be found at www.gayice.is.

MAPS

Free city maps are available from the tourist office, airport, long-distance bus terminal and accommodation throughout Reykjavík, as are free tourist maps of Iceland in general. More detailed road atlases and hiking maps are for sale at the tourist office and in bookshops, and also at some petrol stations. These are usually published by IÐNÚ Publishing, who have a specialist map shop at Brautarholt 8 (tel: 517 7210; www.idnu.is, https://mapoficeland.com; Mon–Fri 10am–4pm). Their maps include the excellent 1:500,000 touring map *Ferðakort Ísland* and the 1:200,000 Ísland Vegaatlas (Road Atlas); five touring maps that cover the country at a scale of 1:250,000 (*Northwest*; *Northeast*; *Southwest*; *Southeast*; and the *Highlands*); and nine 'special' maps, including 1:200,000 maps of *The Golden Circle* (see page 67), *Snæfellsnes/Borgarfjörður* (see page 77) and the *Vestmannaeyjar* (see page 85).

MEDIA

Newspapers and magazines. UK and US newspapers and magazines are available in Reykjavík one or two days after publication, in bookshops and public libraries. The *Reykjavík Grapevine* (http://grapevine.is), an irreverent, free English-language newspaper containing articles, reviews and listings, is published fortnightly March to October, and monthly November to February, and is widely available. The subscription-based magazine *Iceland Review* (www.iceland review.com) is published in English six times per year, with articles and great photographs.

TV. The state-run RÚV channels and the pay channel Stöð 2 are the most widely watched home-grown TV channels in Iceland. Some hotels offer satellite TV with international news and entertainment channels including CNN and BBC Worldwide.

MONEY (See also Budgeting for your trip)

Currency. The Icelandic currency is the króna (ISK; plural: krónur). Notes are in denominations of ISK10,000, 5,000, 2,000, 1,000 and 500, coins in ISK100, 50, 10, 5 and 1.

US dollars, sterling and euros are all easily exchanged at banks. Outside normal banking hours, you can exchange money at major hotels. There are exchange facilities at Keflavík Airport, where the Arion Bank is open from 4am to 8pm, and to coincide with any flights outside these times, in the arrival and departure halls.

At the time of going to press, the rate of exchange was as follows: £1 = ISK143; €1 = ISK127; $1 = ISK109.

Credit and debit cards. Credit and debit cards are used everywhere in Iceland, for even the smallest purchases. US visitors should note that Iceland uses the chip-and-PIN system: double check before travelling that your card will work.

VAT refund. Visitors can claim tax back on purchases as long as they have spent a minimum of ISK6,000 in one transaction – see page 93 for details.

O

OPENING TIMES

Banks: Mon–Fri 9.15am–4pm.

Offices: Mon–Fri 9am–5pm (June–Aug 8am–4pm).
Shops: Mon–Fri 9am–5pm/6pm, Sat 10am–1pm/2pm/3pm/4pm. Some supermarkets open until 11pm daily.
Off licences (liquor stores): Mon–Thu 11am–6pm, Fri 11am–7pm, Sat 11am–6pm. Off licences outside of Reykjavík usually keep much shorter hours – see www.vinbudin.is for details.

P

POLICE

The police keep a low profile, and you are unlikely to come across them unless you commit an offence. They normally speak English.
Emergency police number (also fire and ambulance): tel: 112.

Reykjavík police headquarters is at Hverfisgata 113–115, tel: 444 1000. For lost property, tel. 444 1000. You can also check the police's lost-and-found pinterest: www.pinterest.co.uk/logreglan.

POST OFFICES

The Icelandic postal service is efficient. It takes up to five days for post to reach Europe or North America and 10 days for Australia, New Zealand and South Africa. In shock news, the main Reykjavík post office was due to leave its 150-year-old home on Pósthússtræti in November 2018, relocating out of the city centre to Hagatorg (just southwest of the National Museum) – ask the tourist office or check www.postur.is for the new location and opening times (previously Mon–Fri 9am–6pm).

At the time of publication, a first class (A-póstur) letter weighing less than 50g (1.7oz) cost ISK225 to Europe and ISK285 to the rest of the world. There are up-to-date prices and further information at www.postur.is.

PUBLIC HOLIDAYS

Most businesses, banks and shops close on public holidays, and public transport is limited.

Fixed dates:

1 January New Year's Day

1 May Labour Day

17 June National Day

24 December Christmas Eve (from noon)

25 December Christmas Day

26 December Boxing Day

31 December New Year's Eve (from noon)

Movable dates:

Maundy Thursday

Good Friday

Easter Sunday

Easter Monday

First day of summer (first Thursday after 18 April)

Ascension Day

Whit Sunday

Whit Monday

Bank Holiday Monday (first Monday in August)

R

RELIGION

Eighty percent of the population are Lutheran, and there are churches and chapels all over the country, even on some farms. Four percent are Catholic. As always, dress modestly and be respectful when looking around churches and cathedrals.

Reykjavík has two cathedrals. Dómkirkjan, the Protestant cathedral (Austurvöllur; http://domkirkjan.is), holds communion services on Sunday at 11am. Kathólska Kirkjan, the Catholic cathedral (Túngata 13; www.catholica.is), celebrates Mass in English on Sunday at 6pm. At Hallgrímskirkja (Skólavörðuholt; www.hallgrimskirkja.is), Sunday Mass is held at 11am.

T

TELEPHONES

The code for Iceland is +354, followed by a seven-digit number. There are no area codes. If you use the Iceland telephone book, remember that it lists people by their first names.

To call abroad from Iceland, dial 00, followed by the code of the country you are calling.

The cheapest way to make local calls is to buy an Icelandic SIM card and use it in your (unlocked) mobile phone. Pre-paid SIM cards, from providers Nova, Síminn and Vodafone, can be bought at petrol stations, 10/11 shops and some hotels and tourist offices. Síminn is slightly more expensive, but has the best countrywide coverage. Its starter pack costs ISK2,900 and contains a combined mini/micro/nano SIM card that gives you 50 minutes of calls and 50 texts to Icelandic numbers, plus five GB of data. You can top up the SIM card by following the instructions in the starter pack. Credit expires six months after you last use it.

US visitors should check before leaving home whether their phones will work on the GSM 900/1800 network.

Useful numbers are as follows:

118: directory enquiries

1811: international directory enquiries

TIME ZONES

Iceland is on gmt all year round. This means that it has the same time as the UK from the last Sunday in October to the last Sunday in March; and is one hour behind the UK the rest of the year.

New York	**Reykjavík**	London	Sydney	Auckland
8am	**noon**	1pm	10pm	midnight

TIPPING

Service is always included, so tipping is not necessary in Iceland.

TOILETS

Public toilets in Reykjavík look like round green columns, covered in advertisements – in the city centre, there's one on Ingólfstorg, one near Kólaportið flea market (on the corner of Tryggvagata and Naustin) and one near Hallgrímskirkja (at the top of Frakkastígur). As they are rather limited in number, it's probably easiest to buy a coffee at a bar or café and use the toilets as a patron.

Outside Reykjavík, a recent spate of tourists doing their business in public places has disgusted Icelanders. Plan bathroom breaks, and be prepared to pay a small bathroom charge (ISK200 to ISK400) if necessary, in cafés, petrol stations and at sights such as those on the Golden Circle tour.

TOURIST INFORMATION

Visit Reykjavík runs the official Tourist Information Centre (Tjarnargata 1; tel: 411 6040; www.visitreykjavik.is; daily 8am–8pm) inside City Hall, next to Tjörnin lake. Staff speak excellent English and usually provide helpful information. The centre has free maps and brochures, as well as free Wi-fi, and sells hiking maps, travel guides and tour tickets, plus tickets for the Flybus and the local Strætó bus service. There are also numerous private tourist offices in the city.

If you're planning to explore a little further afield, the websites for the six official regional tourist boards are: Visit West Iceland (www. west.is), Visit Westfjords (www.westfjords.is), Visit North Iceland (www. northiceland.is), Visit East Iceland (www.east.is), Visit South Iceland (www.south.is), Visit Reykjanes (www.visitreykjanes.is).

Inspired by Iceland (www.inspiredbyiceland.com) promotes Iceland abroad. Its website is a mine of information about Icelandic history, geology, people and culture. It also provides travel advice and regional information, and has a large database of activities, tours and accommodation, from camping to top-class hotels.

TRANSPORT

Buses (city). Reykjavík has an excellent bus system, run by Strætó. Its yellow city buses generally run Mon–Fri 6.30am–11.30pm, Sat 7.30am–11.30pm and Sun 9.30am–11.30pm. A single ticket costs ISK460, or a one/three-day pass costs ISK1,700/4,000. When you get on the bus, you need to have a pre-bought bus pass or bus ticket, or the exact fare in cash (city buses don't take debit or credit cards, or give change). If you are changing buses, ask for a *skiftimiði* (exchange ticket), which is valid on all buses for 75 minutes. Route maps are available from tourist offices and at www.straeto.is. The Strætó app, for Android and iPhones, allows you to buy tickets in-app (when you want to travel, activate the ticket, then show the screen to the driver as you board), and check bus times and connections in real time. Children under six travel free, and there are reduced fares for under 18 year olds.

Buses (long distance). Some (yellow-and-blue) Strætó buses drive to destinations outside the capital – most leave from Mjódd terminal, 8km (5 miles) southeast of the city centre. Long-distance buses operate from BSÍ Bus Terminal (Vatnsmýrarvegur; tel: 562 1011, www.bsi. is). In summer, Reykjavík Excursions offers various long-distance bus passes – see Iceland on your Own (tel: 580 5400, www.re.is/iceland-on-your-own) for prices and schedules.

Domestic flights. Air Iceland Connect (tel: 570 3030, www.airicelandconnect.com), the biggest domestic carrier, runs direct flights from Reykjavík's domestic airport to Akureyri, Egilsstaðir and Ísafjörður. Flights are often cheaper than buses, especially if you can travel light (with hand luggage only, weighing under 6kg/13lbs).

Eagle Air (Flugfélagið Ernir, tel: 562 2640, www.eagleair.is) also operates internal flights from Reykjavík to Bíldudalur and Gjögur in the West Fjords, Húsavík, Höfn and the Vestmannaeyjar.

Ferries. The ferry *Herjólfur* (tel: 481 2800, www.saeferdir.is) runs to the Vestmannaeyjar from Landeyjahöfn near Hvollsvöllur on the south coast (or sometimes from Þorlákshöfn in certain wind/tide conditions).

There are six sailings per day in high summer, and four in winter, taking 35 minutes in good conditions. The return trip for a foot passenger costs ISK2,760.

Taxis. Taxis are available in all major towns and cost about ISK2,300 for 3km (1.9 miles). There are ranks in Reykjavík on Lækjargata and Eiríksgata (alongside Hallgrímskirkja), but to avoid queueing most people book one of the four 24-hour cab companies by phone: Airport Taxi (tel: 420 1212, www.airporttaxi.is); Borgarbílastöðin (tel: 552 2440, www.borgarbilastodin.is); BSR (tel: 561 0000, www.taxi reykjavik.is); or Hreyfill (tel: 588 5522, www.hreyfill.is).

V

VISAS AND ENTRY REQUIREMENTS

Iceland has signed the Schengen Agreement, so, in principle, residents of other Schengen countries (Norway plus all EU countries except Britain and Ireland) can enter the country using national identity cards rather than passports. Flights from the UK require passengers to go through passport control. Iceland doesn't require visas from citizens of EU states, the US, Canada, Australia or New Zealand; South African citizens do require one. The normal entry stamp in your passport is valid for a stay of up to 90 days, and your passport must be valid for a further three months beyond your proposed departure date. See www.utl.is for further information.

W

WEBSITES AND INTERNET ACCESS

In addition to the websites listed in the sections above, the following provide useful and/or interesting background information:

https://guidetoiceland.is (marketplace for over 1,000 Icelandic travel operators) www.iceland.is (promotes Icelandic culture, nature, economy, travel and leisure)

https://icelandmusic.is (directory of festivals, gigs, record shops etc)

www.sagatrail.is (museums and historical sites connected to the Icelandic Sagas)

https://ust.is/the-environment-agency-of-iceland (information about Iceland's national parks and conservation areas)

https://en.vedur.is/weather/forecasts/aurora (Northern Lights forecast)

www.whatson.is (Reykjavík calendar of events)

Wi-fi is widely available (free) in cafés, bars and N1 petrol stations. Hotels, guesthouses, libraries and tourist-information offices often have computers with an internet connection that you can use free or for a small charge.

Y

YOUTH HOSTELS

Hostelling International Iceland (www.hostel.is) has 34 excellent hostels from which to choose, including three in Reykjavík, all open year-round. Reykjavík Downtown HI Hostel (Vesturgata 17, tel: 553 8120, reykjavikdowntown@hostel.is) and Reykjavík Loft HI Hostel (Bankastræti 7, tel: 553 8140, loft@hostel.is) are slap-bang in the city centre, while Reykjavík City HI Hostel (Sundlaugavegur 34, 105 Reykjavík, tel: 553 8110, reykjavikcity@hostel.is) is approximately 2.5km (1.5 miles) east of the action, close to Laugardalslaug swimming pool. HI hostels are inordinately popular and fill up quickly in summer – make sure you book ahead. Most hostels have two- to six-bed dorm rooms and family rooms, and good facilities including self-catering kitchens, laundry facilities and free Wi-fi. You can use your own sleeping-bag/linen or hire what you need.

RECOMMENDED HOTELS

Reykjavík's hotels generally offer a good standard of accommodation, although you might expect more space, personality and general pizzazz for the often eye-watering prices that you pay. Rooms are usually perfectly comfortable and clean, with all the fittings, but bland: there are a lot of modern minimalist interiors out there, all with the same pale wooden floors, cream duvets and chrome fittings, which may leave you pining for a touch of old-world charm and character.

Guesthouses in Reykjavík often represent better value for money, though their rooms are naturally not as well-appointed as those of the city's higher-end hotels. There is often little to choose between guesthouses. Should you opt to stay in one, location will probably be your deciding factor.

Breakfast may or may not be included in the room rate of hotels or guesthouses – check when you book. If not, it generally costs around ISK1,500–2,500 extra.

Even in the top hotels, thin walls and curtains are common – light sleepers are advised to bring earplugs and an eye mask.

Early online bookings are recommended for high season (mid-May to mid-September), when prices often double and rooms can be hard to come by, as the huge influx of visitors has left hotels and guesthouses struggling to cope. Indeed, seemingly everywhere you look in Reykjavík, you'll see another hotel going up to cater for the ever-expanding tourist industry.

Price guidelines below are for a double room with bathroom in high season, unless otherwise stated. Hotels usually accept payment by credit card; payment for some guesthouses may be cash-only.

$$$$	over ISK30,000
$$$	ISK24,000–30,000
$$	ISK17,000–24,000
$	below ISK17,000

Alba Guesthouse $ *Eskihlíð 3, tel: 552 9800*, www.alba.is. Near the long-distance bus station, Alba has 10 trim and tidy rooms with shared bathrooms. It's particularly good value as a buffet-style breakfast is included in the room price.

Álfhóll Guesthouse $$ *Ránargata 8, tel: 898 1838*, www.alfholl.is. A cosy little guesthouse a short distance from the centre, with clean, comfortable rooms and shared bathrooms. The name means 'Elf Hill', and the owners are always more than happy to tell you all you need to know about Iceland's hidden people.

Arcturus Guesthouse $$ *Sólvallagata 20, tel: 770 4629*, www.arcturus.is. Named after the brightest star in the northern sky, Arcturus is a spotlessly kept place, a smidgen west of the city centre in a quiet residential district. Its plain but pleasant rooms are a decent size; all have shared bathrooms. There's a guest kitchen with fridge and microwave, and free parking is available.

Baldursbrá Guesthouse $$ *Laufasvegur 41, tel: 552 6646*, baldursbra@centrum.is. Kindly French hosts and their delightful dachshunds give guests a warm welcome at this cosy little guesthouse, halfway between the city centre and the long-distance bus station. There's a good ratio of shared bathrooms to rooms, and a hot tub in the back yard.

Hótel Borg $$$$ *Pósthússtræti 11, tel: 551 1440*, www.hotelborg.is. This imposing building near the Icelandic Parliament was the country's first hotel and is a national institution. Rooms are beautifully renovated in modern style, with nods to its Art Deco heritage. Has a small basement spa and fitness studio.

Castle House Luxury Apartments $$ *Skálholtsstígur 2a, tel: 511 2166*, http://hotelsiceland.net. A home-from-home close to the eastern shore of the city lake Tjörnin, these eight self-catering apartments have spacious sitting rooms and bedrooms, bathrooms with heated flooring and well-stocked kitchenettes, as well as phones with free local calls. The same people run the equally excellent Embassy Luxury Apartments, on a quiet street on the western side of the lake.

CenterHotel Þingholt $$$$ *Þingholtsstræti 3-5, tel: 595 8530,* www.centerhotels.com. The best of Reykjavík's six (soon to be eight) Center-Hotel properties, Þingholt has a cool, minimalist style: the lobby is particularly atmospheric, with its black lava wall and tiling made from fish leather. There's an excellent restaurant, and the option of a 4–7am breakfast for early travellers. Its very central location means weekend party noise can be loud – bring earplugs!

Eyja Guldsmeden $$$$ *Brautarholt 10, tel: 519 7300,* www.hoteleyja.is. Any faint concerns about the unglamorous street dissolve upon entering this cosy boutique hotel, a 10-minute walk from the heart of town. All rooms contain simple wooden four-poster beds, softened with fluffy bedspreads and darkened by blackout curtains. Bathroom products are eco-friendly.

Freyja Guesthouse & Suites $$$ *Freyjugata 39, tel: 615 9555,* www.freyjaguesthouse.com. A beautiful little spot, packed with personality and charm and just one street away from Hallgrimskirkja, Freyja has four double rooms, two queens, two singles and a family-of-four studio to choose from – all are delightful. There's also a well-stocked guest kitchen and comfy lounge area; in summer, there are free bicycles for guests to use, too.

Hótel Holt $$$$ *Bergstaðastræti 37, tel: 552 5700,* www.holt.is. A long-standing luxury hotel, famous for its superb restaurant and artworks, which form the largest private collection of Icelandic paintings in existence. Decor is very traditional – think leather, dark woodwork and quiet lounge areas.

Icelandair Hotel Reykjavík Marina $$$$ *Mýrargata 2, tel: 444 4000, 560 8000,* www.icelandairhotels.com. This Icelandair hotel has a laidback ambience, quirky contemporary decoration and harbour views. It's worth splashing out for one of the larger deluxe rooms. The hotel bar Slippbarinn is a celebrated nightspot, with live music and weekend DJs.

Igdlo Guesthouse $ *Gunnarsbraut 46, tel: 511 4646,* http://igdlo.com. This budget option, near the long-distance bus terminal, has three floors of simple rooms with shared bathrooms (although all rooms have sinks).

Handy facilities include a great shared kitchen on the top floor, a washing machine free for guest use and ample free street parking.

Hotel Krúnes $$ *Krúnesvegur 12, 203 Kópavogur, tel: 567 2245*, www. kriunes.is. This tastefully converted, family-run former farmhouse has an absolutely delightful setting beside Lake Elliðaárvatn and Heiðmörk nature reserve. Its new rooms are the best, with big windows that make the most of the views. Offering peace and quiet galore, it's just a 15-minute drive to the city sights.

Kvosin $$$$ *Kirkjutorg 4, tel: 571 4460*, http://kvosinhotel.is. These 24 gorgeous suites, tucked behind the Dómkirkja cathedral, boast the largest bedrooms in Reykjavík. Packed with high-spec features and fittings, each has a kitchenette and either a private balcony or a rooftop deck. A portion of the profits from the Valkyrie suite goes to support Icelandic Paralympians and other athletes with disabilities.

Hótel Leifur Eríksson $$$ *Skólavörðustígur 45, tel: 562 0800*, www.hotel leifur.is. A friendly family-run place with a prime location right opposite Hallgrímskirkja church. Rooms are basic but comfortable. There is no restaurant, although a continental breakfast is included and hot drinks are available 24 hours a day.

Loft Hostel $$ *Bankastræti 7, tel: 553 8140*, www.lofthostel.is. Loft is the newest of the three HI Iceland youth hostels in Reykjavík, with sunny staff, a café-bar and rooftop deck with fabulous city views, plus free events like painting nights, pub quizzes and Sunday yoga. Dorm beds and private rooms available.

Óðinsvé $$$$ *Þórsgata 1, tel: 511 6200*, www.hotelodinsve.is. A relaxed atmosphere and excellent staff make this hotel, in a quiet residential quarter close to the centre, a comfortable place to stay. Standard rooms are a little spartan, but the apartment-like split-level deluxe rooms are very nice indeed.

Reykjavik Residence Hotel $$$$ *Hverfisgata 45, tel: 561 1200*, www. rrhotel.is. For beauty, elegance and a high level of service, look no further than the Reykjavik Residence Hotel. The apartments, scattered across three historic buildings, range from small studios to the suites where King Christian X and Queen Alexandrina of Denmark stayed in 1926.

Room with a View $$$$ *Laugavegur 18, tel: 552 7262,* www.roomwith aview.is. For a good, cost-effective alternative to a hotel, try these comfortable serviced apartments on the main shopping street. The 44 options range from small basement studios to a 12-bed beast – check the website for further details.

Storm Hótel $$$ *Þórunnartún 4, tel: 518 3000,* www.keahotels.is. A new, stylish, modern place, with lots of glass, polished hardwood floors, cool colours and soothing photographs of Iceland's scenery. Located in Reykjavík's business district, a 10-minute walk from the city centre.

Guesthouse Sunna $$ *Þórsgata 26, tel: 511 5570,* https://sunna.is. In a perfect central location, Sunna offers a choice of simple, bright, clean rooms with private or shared bathrooms, and one- and two-bedroom apartments, many with views of Hallgrímskirkja. There are fridges and kettles in the shared kitchenettes on every floor.

Three Sisters Guesthouse $$ *Ránargata 16, tel: 565 2181,* www.threesis ters.is. A splendid alternative to a hotel room, these cosy studio apartments, in a peaceful old house, come with small kitchenettes. The area, near the harbour, is very quiet, yet just a few strides away from the city-centre action.

DICTIONARY

adj lo. **adv** ao. **BE** bresk enska **n** no. **prep** fs. **v** so.

A

accept v **samþykkja [samthickja]**

access n aðgangur [athgoungur]

accident slys [slis]

accommodation húsnæði [hoosnaythi]

account n **(bank)** reikningur [reykneangur]

acupuncture nálastungulækningar [noulastoongulaykneangar]

adapter millistykki [millistikki]

address n heimilisfang [heymilisfoung]

admission (price) aðgangseyrir [athgoungseyrir]

after eftir [eftir] **~noon** síðdegi [seathdeghi] **--shave** rakspíri [rakspeari]

age n aldur [aldur]

agency umboðsskrifstofa [umbothskrifstofa]

AIDS eyðni [eythni]

air n loft [loft] **~ conditioning** loftræsting [loftraysteang] **--dry** loftþurrka [loftthurrka] **~ pump** loftdæla [loftdayla] **~line** flugfélag [flughfyelagh] **~mail** flugpóstur [flughpohstur] **~plane** flugvél [flughvyel] **~port** flugvöllur [flughvuhddlur]

aisle gangur [goungur] **~ seat** gangsæti [goungsayti]

allergic með ofnæmi [meth ofnaymi] **~ reaction** ofnæmisviðbrögð [ofnaymisvithbrunghth]

allow leyfa [leyfa]

alone einn [eydn]

alter v breyta [breyta]

alternate route önnur leið [uhnnur leith]

aluminum foil álpappír [oulpappear]

amazing furðulegur [furthulegur]

ambulance sjúkrabíll [sjookrabeaddl]

American adj bandarískur [bandareaskur]

amusement park skemmtigarður [skemmtigarthur]

anemic blóðlaus [blohthluys]

anesthesia deyfing [deyfeang]

animal dýr [dear]

ankle ökkli [uhkkli]

antibiotic n sýklalyf [seaklalif]

antiques store fornmunabúð [fornmunabooth]

antiseptic cream sótthreinsandi krem [sohtthreynsandi krem]

apartment íbúð [eabooth]

appendix (body part) botnlangi [botnloungi]

appetizer forréttur [forryettur]

appointment stefnumót [stebnumoht]

arcade spilasalur [spilasalur]

area code svæðisnúmer [svæthisnoomer]

arm n **(body part)** handleggur [handleggur]

aromatherapy ilmolíumeðferð [ilmoleaumethferth]

around (the corner) kringum [kreangum] **~ (price)** um það bil [um thath bil]

arrival koma [koma]

arrive koma [koma]

artery slagæð [slagayð]

arthritis liðagigt [lithaghight]

art list [list]

Asian adj asiskur [aseaskur]

aspirin aspirín [aspírean]

asthmatic með asma [meth asma]

ATM hraðbanki [hrathbanki] **~ card** hraðbankakort [hrathbankakort]

attack v ráðast á [routhast ou]

attraction (place) ferðamannastaður [ferthamannastathur]

attractive aðlaðandi [athlathandi]

Australia Ástralía [Oustraleaa]

Australian adj ástralskur [oustralskur]

automatic sjálfvirkur [sjoulfvirkur] **~ car** sjálfskiptur bíll [sjoulfskiftur beaddl]

available fáanlegur [fouanleghur]

B

baby barn [bardn] **~ bottle** peli [peli] **~ wipe** þurrka [thurrka] **~sitter** barnfóstra [bardnfohstra]

back (body part) bak [bak] **~ache** bakverkur [bakverkur] **~pack** bakpoki [bakpoki]

bag poki [poki]

baggage (BE) farangur [faroungur] **~ claim** farangursafgreiðsla [faroungursafgreythsla] **~ ticket** farangursmerki [faroungursmerki]

bake v baka [baka]

bakery bakarí [bakarea]

ballet ballett [ballett]

bandage sáraumbúðir [souraumboothir]

bank n banki [banki]

bar (place) bar [bar]

barbecue (device) n grill [grill]

barber rakari [rakari]

baseball hornabolti [hordnabolti]

basket (grocery store) karfa [karfa]

basketball körfubolti [kuhrvubolti]

bathroom baðherbergi [bathherbergi]

battery rafhlaða [rafhlatha]

battleground vígvöllur [veagvuhddlur]

be v vera [vera]

beach strönd [struhnd]
beautiful fallegur [faddleghur] ~ **falleg** [faddlegh]
bed n rúm [room] ~ **and breakfast** gistiheimili [gistiheymili]
before fyrir [firir]
begin byrja [birja]
beginner byrjandi [birjandi]
behind (direction) fyrir aftan [firir aftan]
beige adj drapplitaður [drapplitathur]
belt belti [belti]
best adj bestur [bestur] ~ **before** best fyrir [best fyrir]
better betri [betri]
bicycle reiðhjól [reithhjol]
big stór [stohr] ~**ger** stærri [stayrri]
bike route reiðhjólastígur [reithhjohlasteaghur]
bikini bikini [bikinea]
bill n (money) seðill [sethiddl] ~ n (of sale) reikningur [reyknaangur]
bird fugl [fugl]
birthday afmælisdagur [afmylisdaghur]
black adj svartur [svartur]
bladder blaðra [blathra]
bland blanda [blanda]
blanket teppi [teppi]
bleed blæða [blaytha]
blender blandari [blandari]
blood blóð [blohth]
~ **pressure** blóðþrýstingur [blohththreasteangur]
blouse blússa [bloossa]
blue adj blár [blour]
board v fara um borð [fara um borth] ~**ing pass** brottfararspjald [brottfararspjald]
boat n bátur [boutur]
boil v sjóða [sjohtha]
bone n bein [beyn]
book n bók [bohk] ~**store** bókabúð [bohkabooth]

boot n stígvél [steagyvel]
boring leiðinlegur [leythinleghur]
botanical garden grasagarður [grasagarthur]
bother v bróðir [brohthir]
bottle n flaska [flaska] ~ **opener** upptakari [upptakari]
bowl n skál [skoul]
boxing match hnefaleikakeppni [hnefaleykakeppni]
boy drengur [dreyngur] ~**friend** kærasti [kayrasti]
bra brjóstahaldari [brjohstahaldari]
bracelet armband [armband]
brake (car) bremsa [bremsa]
breaded i raspi [ea raspi]
break v (bone) brjóta [brjohta]
breakdown (car) bilun [bilun]
breakfast n morgunverður [morgunverthur]
break-in (burglary) innbrot [innbrot]
breast brjóst [brjohst] ~**feed** v brjóstagjof [brjohstagjuhf]
breathe anda [anda]
bridge brú [broo]
briefs (clothing) stuttar nærbuxur [stuttar nayrbuxur]
bring koma með [koma meth]
British adj breskur [breskur]
broken brotinn [brotinn] ~ **(bone)** brotið [brotith]
brooch næla [nayla]
broom kústur [koostur]
brother bróðir [brohthir]
brown adj brúnn [broonn]
bug (insect) n padda [padda]
building bygging [biggeang]

burn v brenna [brenna]
bus n strætó [straytoh] ~ **station** strætóstöð [straytohstuhth] ~ **stop** stoppistöð [stoppistuhth] ~ **ticket** strætómiði [straytohmithi] ~ **tour** strætóleið [straytohleyth]
business adj viðskipti [vithskifti] ~ **card** nafnspjald [nabnspjald] ~ **center** viðskiptamiðstöð [vithskiftamithstuhth] ~ **class** viðskiptafarrými [vithskiftafarreami] ~ **hours** opnunartími [opnunarteami]
butcher n slátrari [sloutrari]
buttocks rass [rass]
buy v kaupa [kuypa]
bye bless [bless]

C

cabaret kabarett [kabarett]
cable car kláfferja [kloufferja]
cafe (place) kaffihús [kaffihoos]
call v (phone) hringja [hreangja] ~ n simtal [seamtal] ~ **collect** hringja á kostnað viðtakanda [hreangja ou kostnath vithtakanda]
calorie hitaeining [hitaeyneang]
camera myndavél [mindavyel] ~ **case** myndavélataska [myndavyelataska] **digital** ~ stafræn myndavél [stafrayn myndavyel]
camp v tjalda [tjalda] ~**ing stove** suðutæki [suthutayki] ~**site** tjaldsvæði [tjaldsvaythi]
can opener dósahnífur [dohsahneafur]
Canada Kanada [Kanada]
Canadian adj kanadiskur

[kanadeaskur]
cancel hætta við [haytta vith]
candy sælgæti [saylgayti]
canned good niðursuðuvörur [nithursuthuvuhrur]
canyon gljúfur [gljoofur]
car bíll (beatl) ~ hire (BE) bílaleiga [bealaleygha] ~ **park** (BE) bílastæði [bealastaythi] ~ **rental** bílaleiga [bealaleygha] ~ **seat** bílsæti [bealsayti]
carafe karafla [karafla]
card n kort [kort] **ATM** ~ hraðbankakort [hrathbankakort] **credit** ~ kreditkort [kreditkort] **debit** ~ debetkort [debetkort] **phone** ~ símkort [seamkort]
carry-on n (piece of hand luggage) handfarangur [handfaroungur]
cart (grocery store) kerra [kerra] ~ **(luggage)** farangurskerra [faroungarskerra]
carton (of cigarettes) karton [karton] ~ **(of groceries)** pappakassi [pappakassi]
cash n peningar [peneangar] ~ v skipta [skifta]
cashier gjaldkeri [gjaldkeri]
casino spilavíti [spilaveati]
castle kastali [kastali]
cathedral dómkirkja [dohmkirkja]
cave n hellir [hellir]
CD geisladiskur [geisladiskur]
cell phone farsími [farseami]
Celsius celsíus [celseaus]
centimeter sentimetri [senteametri]
certificate vottorð [vottorth]
chair n stóll [stohddl]

~ **lift** stólalyfta [stohlalifta]
change v **(baby)** skipta á [skifta ou] ~ **(buses)** skipta um [skifta um] ~ **(money)** skipta [skifta] ~ n **(money)** afgangur [afgoungur]
charge v **(credit card)** skuldfæra [skuldfayra] ~ **(cost)** verð [verth]
cheap ódýrt [ohdeart] ~er ódýrara [ohdearara]
check v **(luggage)** innrita [innrita] ~ **(on something)** athuga [athugha] n **(payment)** athugun [athughun] ~**in** innritun [innritun] ~**ing account** tékkareikningur [tyeckareykneangur] ~**out** útskráning [ootskrouneang]
Cheers! skál! [skoul!]
chemical toilet efnaklósett [ebnaklohsett]
chemist [BE] apótekari [apohtekari]
chest (body part) bringa [breanga] ~ **pain** brjóstverkur [brjohstverkur]
chewing gum tyggigummi [tyggigoommea]
child barn [bardn] ~**'s seat** barnastóll [bardnastohddl]
children's menu barnamatseðill [bardnamatsethill]
children's portion barnaskammtur [bardnaskammtur]
Chinese adj kínverskur [keanverskur]
chopsticks matprjónar [matprjohnar]
church matprjónn [matprjohnn]
cigar vindill [vindiddl]

class n farrými [farreami]
business ~ viðskipta-farrými [vithskiftafar-

reami] **economy** ~ almennt farrými [almennt farreami] **first** ~ fyrsta farrými [fyrsta farreami]
classical music klassísk tónlist [klasseask tohnlist]
clean v hreinsa [hreynsa] ~ adj **(clothes)** hrein [hreyn] ~**ing product** hreinsivara [hreynsivara]
clear v **(on an ATM)** hreinsa [hreynsa]
cliff bjarg [bjarg]
cling film [BE] umbúða-filma [umboothafilma]
close v **(a shop)** loka [loka]
closed lokuð [lokuth]
clothing föt [fuht] ~ **store** fataverslun [fataverslun]
club n klúbbur [kloobbur]
coat yfirhöfn [ifirhuhbn]
coin mynt [mint]
colander dörslag [duhrslag]
cold n **(sickness)** kvef [kvef] ~ adj **(temperature)** kaldur [kaldur]
colleague samstarfsmaður [samstarfsmathur]
cologne ilmvatn [ilmvatn]
color n litur [litur]
comb n greiða [greitha]
come v koma [koma]
complaint kvarta [kvarta]
computer tölva [tuhlva]
concert tónleikar [tohnlei-kar] ~ **hall** tónlistarhús [tohnlistarhoos]
condition (medical) ástand [oustand]
conditioner (hair) hárnæring [hournay-reang]
condom smokkur [smockur]
conference ráðstefna [routhstebna]
confirm samþykkja [samthickja]
congestion (medical)

stífla [steafla]
connect (internet) tengja [teyngja]
connection (travel/internet) teng-ing [teyngeang] ~ **flight** tengiflug [teynghiflugh]
constipated með hægðatregðu [meth haygthatregthu]
consulate ræðismanns-skrifstofa [raythis-mannsskrifstofa]
consultant ráðgjafi [routhgjafi]
contact v hafa samband [hafa samband]
contact lens augnlinsa [augnlinsa] ~ **solution** augnlinsulausn [uygnlin-suluysn]
contagious smitandi [smitandi]
convention hall ráðstefnusalur [routh-stebnusalur]
conveyor belt færiband [fayriband]
cook v elda [elda]
cool adj **(temperature)** svalur [svalur]
copper n kopar [kopar]
corkscrew v korktappi [korktappi]
cost v kosta [kosta]
cotton bómull [bohmull]
cough v hósta [hohsta] ~ n hósti [hohsti]
country code landsnúmer [landsnoomer]
cover charge aðgangseyrir [athgoungseyrir]
cream (ointment) krem [krem]
credit card kreditkort [kreditkort]
crew neck stroffhálsmál [stroffhoulsmoul]
crib barnarúm [bardna-room]
crystal n **(glass)** kristall [kristall]
cup n bolli [bolli]

currency gjaldmiðill [gjaldmithill] ~ **exchange** gjaldeyrisviðskipti [gjaldeyrisvithskifti] ~ **exchange office** gjaldeyrisskiptastöð [gjaldeyrisskiftastuhth]
current account [BE] ávísanareikningur [ou-veasanareykneangur]
customs tollskoðun [toddlskothun]
cut v skera [skera] ~ n **(injury)** skurður [skurthur]
cute sætur [saytur]
cycling hjólreiðar [hjohlreithar]

D

damage v skemma [skemma]
dance v dansa [dansa] ~ **club** dansklúbbur [danskloobbur] ~**ing** dans [dans]
dangerous hættulegur [hayttuleghur]
dark adj dimmt [dimmt]
date n **(calendar)** dagset-ning [daghsetneangh]
day dagur [daghur]
deaf adj heyrnarlaus [heyrdnarluys]
debit card debetkort [debetkort]
deck chair þilfarsstóll [thilfarsstohddl]
declare v **(customs)** tilkynna [tilkinna]
decline v **(credit card)** hafna [habna]
deep adj djúpur [djuhpur]
degree (temperature) gráða [groutha]
delay n töf [tuhf]
delete v **(computer)** eyða [eytha]
delicatessen sælkerafæði [saylkerafaythi]
delicious ljúffengt [ljuhffeyngt]

denim denim [deneam]
dentist tannlæknir
[tannlayknir]
denture gervigómur
[gervigohmur]
deodorant svitalyktareyðir
[svitaliktareithir]
department store
deildaskipt verslun
[deyldaskift verslun]
departure (plane) brottfór
[brottfuhr]
deposit v **(money)**
leggja inn [leggja inn]
~ n **(bank)** innistæða
[innistaytha]
desert n eyðimörk
[eythimuhrk]
detergent þvottaefni
[thvottaebni]
develop v **(film)** framkalla
[framkaddla]
diabetic adj sykursjúkur
[sikursjuhkur] n
sykursýki [sykurseaki]
dial v hringja [hreangja]
diamond demantur
[demantur]
diaper bleyja [bleyja]
diarrhea niðurgangur
[nithurgoungur]
diesel disel [deasel]
difficult erfitt [erfitt]
digital stafrænt [stafraynt]
~ **camera** stafræn
myndavél [stafrayn
myndavvel] ~ **photo**
stafræn ljósmynd
[stafrayn ljohsmynd]
~ **print** stafræn prentun
[stafrayn prentun]
dining room borðsalur
[borthsalur]
dinner kvöldmatur
[kvuhldmatur]
direction átt [outt]
dirty skítugur [skeatughur]
disabled adj **(person)**
fatlaður [fatlathur]
~ **accessible** [BE]
aðgangur fyrir fatlaða
[athgoungur fyrir
fatlatha]

disconnect (computer)
aftengja [afteyngja]
discount n afsláttur
[afslouttur]
dishes (kitchen) diskar
[diskar]
dishwasher uppþvottavél
[uppthvottavvel]
dishwashing liquid
uppþvottavélasápa
[uppthvottavvelasoupa]
display n **(device)**
skjár [skjour] ~ **case**
sýningarkassi [seanean-
garkassi]
disposable n einnota [eyn-
nota] ~ **razor** einnota
rakvél [eynnota rakvvel]
dive v kafa [kafa]
diving equipment
kafarabúnaður [kafar-
abuhnathur]
divorce v skilja [skilja]
dizzy adj svima [svima]
doctor n læknir [layknir]
doll n brúða [bruhtha]
dollar (U.S.) dollari
[dollari]
domestic innanlands
[innanlands] ~ **flight**
innanlandsflug [in-
nanlandsflugh]
door hurð [hurth]
dormitory svefnsalur
[svebnsalur]
double bed tvíbreitt rúm
[tveabreytt ruhm]
downtown n miðbær
[mithbayr]
dozen tylft [tilft]
drag lift toglyfta [toghlifta]
dress (clothing) kjóll
[kjohddl] ~ **code**
klæðaburður [klay-
thaburthur]
drink v drekka [drecka]
~ n drykkur [drickur]
~ **menu** drykkjalisti
[drickjalisti] ~ **ing water**
drykkjarvatn [drick-
jarvatn]
drive v aka [aka]
driver's license number

númer ökuskírteinis [nuh-
mer uhkuskearteynis]
drop n **(medicine)** dropi
[dropi]
drowsiness syfja [sifja]
dry clean þurrhreinsa
[thurrhreynsa] ~**er's**
fatahreinsun [fatah-
reynsun]
dubbed uppnefndur
[uppnefndur]
during á meðan [ou
methan]
duty (tax) tollur [toddlur]
~**free** tollfrjáls [tod-
dlfrjouls]
DVD DVD [dje vaff dje]

E

ear eyra [eyra] ~**ache** eyrnaverkur [eyrdnaverkur]
earlier áður [outhur]
early snemma [snemma]
earring eyrnalokkur
[eyrdnalockur]
east n austur [uystur]
easy auðvelt [uythvelt]
eat v borða [bortha]
economy class almennt
farrými [almennt
farreami]
elbow n olnbogi [olnboghi]
electric outlet
rafmagnsinnstunga
[rafmagnsinnstoonga]
elevator lyfta [lifta]
e-mail v senda tölvupóst
[senda tuhlvupohst] ~ n
tölvupóstur [tuhlvupohs-
tur] ~ **address** netfang
[netfoung]
emergency neyðartilvik
[neythartilvik] ~ **exit**
neyðarútgangur
[neytharootgoungur]
empty v tæma [tayma]
end v enda [enda] ~ n endir
[endir]
engaged (person) trúlofaður [truhlofathur]
English adj enskur
[enskur] ~ n **(language)**
enska [enska]

engrave áletra [ouletra]
enjoy njóta [njohta]
enter v **(place)** koma inn
[koma inn]
entertainment skemmtun
[skemmtun]
entrance inngangur
[inngoungur]
envelope umslag
[umslagh]
epileptic adj flogaveikur
[floghaveykur] ~n
flogaveiki [floghaveyki]
equipment tæki [tayki]
escalator rúllustigi [ruhl-
lustighi]
e-ticket rafrænn farseðill
[rafraynn farsetihddl]
EU resident íbúi á
Evrópusambandssvæðinu
[eabuhi ou Evrohpusam-
bandssvaythinu]
euro evra [evra]
evening n kvöld [kvuhld]
excess baggage
umframfarangurs
[umframfaroungurs]
exchange v skipta [skifta]
~ n **(place)** gjaldeyrisskipti [gjaldeyrisskifti]
~ **rate** gengi [geyngi]
excursion skoðunarferð
[skothunarferth]
excuse v afsaka [afsaka]
exhausted uppgefinn
[uppgefinn]
exit v fara út [fara uht] ~ n
útgangur [ootgoungur]
expensive dýr [dear]
experienced reyndur
[reyndur]
expert sérfræðingur
[syerfraytheangur]
exposure (film) lýsing
[leaseang]
express adj senda með
hraði [senda meth
hrathi] ~ **bus** hraðvagn
[hrathvagn] ~ **train**
hraðlest [hrathlest]
extension (phone) bein
lína [beyn leana]
extra adj auka [uyka]

~ **large** umframstærð [umframstayrth]

extract v (tooth) draga [draga]

eye n auga [uygha]

eyebrow wax augabrú-navax [uyghabruhnavax]

F

face n andlit [andlit]

facial n andlitssnyrting [andlitssnyrteang]

family n fjölskylda [fjuhlskylda]

fan n (appliance) vifta [vifta]

far (distance) langt í burtu [loungt ea burtu]

farm bóndabær [bohndabayr]

far-sighted fjarsýnn [fjarseann]

fast adj fljótur [fljohtur]

fat free fitulaus [fituluys]

father faðir [fathir]

fax v faxa [faxa] ~ n fax [fax] ~ **number** faxnúmer [faxnoomer]

fee n gjald [gjald]

feed v mata [mata]

ferry n ferja [ferja]

fever n hiti [hiti]

field (sports) völlur [vuhddlur]

fill v (car) fylla [filla]

fill out v (form) fylla út [fiddla uht]

filling n (tooth) fylling [fiddleang]

film n (camera) filma [filma]

fine n (fee for breaking law) sekt [sekt]

finger n fingur [feangur] ~**nail** fingurnögl [feangurnuhgl]

fire n eldur [eldur] ~ **department** slökkvilið [sluhckvilith] ~ **door** eldvarnarhurð [eldvarnarhurth]

first adj fyrstur [firstur] ~ **class** fyrsta farrými

[fyrsta farreami]

fit n (clothing) passa [passa]

fitting room mátunarklefi [moutunarklefi]

fix v (repair) laga [lagha]

fixed-price menu matseðill með föstu verði [matsethiddl meth fuhstu verthi]

flash photography flass myndataka [flass mindataka]

flashlight vasaljós [vasaljohs]

flight n flug [flugh]

flip-flops sandali [sandali]

floor n (level) hæð [hayth]

florist blómabúð [blohmabuhth]

flower n blóm [blohm]

folk music þjóðlagatónlist [thjohthlaghatohnlist]

food matur [matur] ~ **processor** matvinnsluvél [matvinnsluvyel]

foot n fótur [fohtur]

football game (BE) fótboltaleikur [fohtbolta-leykur]

for fyrir [firir]

forecast n spá [spou]

forest n skógur [skohghur]

fork n gaffall [gaffaddl]

form n (document) eyðublað [eythublath]

formula (baby) blanda [blanda]

fort virki [virki]

fountain n gosbrunnur [gosbrunnur]

free adj frjáls [frjouls]

freelance work laus-avinna [luysavinna]

freezer frystir [fristir]

fresh ferskur [ferskur]

friend vinur [vinur]

frozen food frosinn matur [frosinn matur]

frying pan steikarpanna [steykarpanna]

full-time adj sívirkur [seavirkur]

G

game n leikur [leykur]

garage n (parking) bílskúr [bealskuhr] ~ n (for repairs) verkstæði [verkstaythi]

garbage bag ruslapoki [ruslapoki]

gas (car) bensín [bensean] ~ **station** bensínstöð [benseanstuhth]

gate (airport) hlið [hlith]

gay adj (homosexual) samkynhneigður [samkinhneighthur] ~ **bar** hommabar [hommabar] ~ **club** hommaklúbbur [hommakloobbur]

gel n (hair) gel [gel]

generic drug samheitalyf [samheitalif]

German adj þýskur [theaskur] ~ n (language) þyska [theaska]

Germany Þýskaland [theaskaland]

get off (a train/bus[subway]) fara úr [fara uhr]

gift n gjöf [gjuhf] ~ **shop** gjafaverslun [gjafaverslun]

girl n stúlka [stuhlka] ~**friend** kærasta [kay-rasta]

give v gefa [gefa]

glass (drinking) glas [glas] ~ (material) gler [gler]

glasses gleraugu [gleruygu]

go v (somewhere) fara [fara]

gold n gull [guddl]

golf n golf [golf] ~ **course** golfvöllur [golfvuhddlur] ~ **tournament** golfmót [golfmoht]

good adj góður [gohthur] ~ n vara [vara] ~ **afternoon** gott kvöld [gott kvuhld] ~ **day** góðan dag [ghohthan dagh]

~ **evening** gott kvöld [gott kvuhld] ~ **morning** góðan dag [gohthan dagh] ~**bye** bless [bless]

gram gramm [gramm]

grandchild barnabarn [bardnabardn]

grandparents amma og afi [amma ogh afi]

gray adj grár [grour]

green adj grænn [graynn]

grocery store matvöruver-slun [matvuhruverslun]

ground floor jarðhæð [jarthhayth]

groundcloth hlífðardúkur [hleafthardurhkur]

group n hópur [hohpur]

guide n (book) leiðarvísir [leytharveasir] ~ n (person) leiðsögumaður [leythsughgumathur] ~ **dog** leiðsöguhundur [leythsughguhundur]

gym n (place) rækt [raykt]

gynecologist kven-sjúkdómafræðingur [kvensjuhkdohmafraytheangur]

H

hair hár [hour] ~**brush** hárbursti [hourbursti] ~**cut** klipping [klippeang] ~ **dryer** hárþurrka [hourthurrka] ~ **salon** hárgreiðslustofa [hourgreythslustofa] ~**spray** hársprey [hoursprey] ~**style** hártíska [hourteaska] ~ **stylist** hársnyrtir [hoursnirtir]

halal leyfilegt [leyfileght]

half adj hálfur [houlfur] ~ n helmingur [helmeangur] ~ **hour** hálftími [houlfteami] ~**kilo** hálft kíló [houlft kealoh]

hammer n hamar [hamar]

hand n hendi [hendi] ~ **luggage** handfarangur [handfaroungur] ~ **wash**

handþvottur [handthvot-
tur] **~bag** [BE]
handtaska [handtaska]
handicapped fatlaður
[fatlathur] **~-acces-
sible** aðgangur fyrir
fatlaða [athgoungur fyrir
fatlatha]
hangover timburmenn
[timburmenn]
happy hamingjusamur
[hameangjusamur]
hat hattur [hattur]
have v hafa [hafa] **~ sex**
stunda kynlíf [stunda
kynleaf]
hay fever heymæði
[heymaythi]
head (body part) n
höfuð [huhfuth]
~ache höfuðverkur
[huhfuthverkur]
~phones heyrnartól
[heyrdnartohl]
health heilsa
[heylsa] **~ food store**
heilsufæðisverslun
[heylsufaythisverslun]
hearing impaired
heyrnarskertur [heyrd-
narskertur]
heart hjarta [hjarta]
~ condition hjartveiki
[hjartveyki]
heat v hita [hita] **~er**
hitari [hitari] **~ing** [BE]
upphitun [upphitun]
hectare hektari [hektari]
hello halló [halloh]
helmet hjálmur [hjoulmur]
help v hjálpa [hjoulpa] **~** v
hjálp [hjoulp]
here hér [hyer]
hi hæ [hay]
high hátt [houtt] **~chair**
hásæti [housayti]
~lights (hair) strípur
[streapur] **~way** þjóðvegur [thjohthveghur]
hiking boots gönguskór
[guhnguskohr]
hill n hæð [hayth]
hire v [BE] **(a car)** taka

bíl á leigu [taka beal
ou leyghu] **~ car**
[BE] bílaleigubifreið
[bealaleyghubifreyth]
hockey hokkí [hockea]
holiday [BE] frí [frea]
horsetrack hestastígur
[hestasteaghur]
hospital sjúkrahús
[sjuhkrahuhs]
hostel farfuglaheimili
[farfuglaheymili]
hot (spicy) sterkur
[sterkur] **~ (tempera-
ture)** heitur [heytur]
~ spring heitur hver
[heytur hver] **~ water**
heitt vatn [heytt vatn]
hotel hótel [hohtel]
hour klukkustund
[kluckustund]
house n hús [huhs] **~hold
goods** heimilisvörur
[heymilisvuhrur] **~keep-
ing services** heimil-
ishald [heymilishald]
how hvernig [hverdnigh]
~ much hve mikið [hve
mikith]
hug v faðma [fathma]
hungry svangur [svoungur]
hurt v meiða [meytha]
husband eiginmaður
[eyghinmathur]

I

ibuprofen íbúprófen
[eabuhprohfen]
ice n ís [eas] **~hockey**
íshokkí [eashockea]
icy ískaldur [easkaldur]
identification auðkenni
[uythkenni]
ill veikur [veykur]
in í [ea]
include v innifela [innifela]
indoor pool (public)
innisundlaug [in-
nisundluygh]
inexpensive ódýr [ohdear]
infected smitaður
[smitathur]
information (phone)

upplýsingar [up-
pleaseangar] **~ desk**
upplýsingaborð [up-
pleaseangaborth]
insect skordýr [skordear]
~ bite skordýrabit
[skordearabit] **~ repel-
lent** skordýraeitur
[skordearaeytur]
insert v **(card)** setja inn
[setja inn]
insomnia svefnleysi
[svebnleysi]
instant message
spjallskilaboð [spjad-
dlskilaboth]
insulin insúlín [insuhlean]
insurance trygging
[triggeang] **~ card**
tryggingarskírteini
[tryggeangarskearteyni]
~ company trygg-
ingafélag [tryggean-
gafyelagh]
interesting áhugavert
[ouhughavert]
intermediate millistig
[middlistigh]
international alþjóðlegur
[althjohthleghur]
~ flight millilandaflug
[middlilandaflugh]
~ student card
alþjóðlegt nemendaskír-
teini [althjohthlegt
nemendaskearteyni]
internet internet [internet]
~ cafe netkaffi-
híhús [netkaffihoos]
~ service netþjónusta
[netthjohnusta]
interpreter túlkur
[tuhlkur]
intersection gatnamót
[gatnamoht]
intestine þarmur [tharmur]
introduce v **(person)**
kynna [kinna]
invoice n [BE] reikningur
[reykneangur]
Ireland Írland [earland]
Irish adj írskur [earskur]
iron v járn [jourdn] **~** n

(clothes) straujárn
[struyjourdn]
Italian adj ítalskur
[eatalskur]

J

jacket n jakki [jacki]
Japanese adj japanskur
[japanskur]
jar n **(for jam etc)** krukka
[krucka]
jaw n kjálki [kjoulki]
jazz n djass [djass]
~ club djassklúbbur
[djasskloobbur]
jeans gallabuxur
[gallabuxur]
jet ski n sæþota [saythota]
jeweler skartgripasali
[skartgripasali]
jewelry skartgripir
[skartgripir]
join v **(go with somebody)** vera samferða
[vera samfertha]
joint n **(body part)** liður
[lithur]

K

key n lykill [likiddl] **~ card**
aðgangskort [athgoung-
skort] **~ring** lyklakippa
[lyklakippa]
kiddie pool barnasundlaug
[bardnasundluygh]
kidney (body part) nýra
[neara]
kilo kíló [kealoh] **~gram**
kílógramm [kealoh-
gramm] **~meter** kílóme-
ter [kealohmeter]
kiss v koss [koss]
kitchen eldhús [eldhuhs]
~ foil [BE] eldhúsfilma
[eldhoosfilma]
knee n hné [hnye]
knife hnífur [hneafur]
kosher adj leyfilegt
[leyfileght]

L

lace n **(fabric)** blúndur
[bluhndur]

lactose intolerant laktósaóþol [laktohs-aohthol]

lake stöðuvatn [stuhthu-vatn]

large stór [stohr]

last adj síðastur [seathastur]

late (time) seinn [seynn]

launderette [BE] þvot-tahús [thvottahuhs]

laundromat þvottavél [thvottavyel]

laundry (place) þvottahús [thvottahuhs] **~ service** þvottabjónusta [thvot-tathjohnusta]

lawyer n lögfræðingur [luhghfraytheanghur]

leather n leður [lethur]

leave v (hotel) fara frá [fara frou] **~ (plane)** fara úr [fara oor]

left adj, adv (direction) vinstri [vinstri]

leg n fótur [fohtur]

lens linsa [linsa]

less minna [minna]

lesson n kennslustund [kennslustund] **take ~s** fara í tíma [fara ea teama]

letter n bréf [bryef]

library bókasafn [bohkasabn]

life jacket björgunarvesti [bjuhrgunarvesti]

lifeguard gæslumaður [gayslumathur]

lift n [BE] lyfta [lifta] **~ (ride)** lyftuferð [lyftuferth] **~ pass** lyftumiði [lyftumithi]

light n (cigarette) kveikja í [kveykja ea] **~** n (overhead) ljós [ljohs] **~bulb** ljósapera [ljohsapera]

lighter n léttari [lyettari]

like v líka við [leaka vith]

line n (train/bus) leið [leyth]

linen rúmföt [ruhmfuht]

lip n vör [vuhr]

liquor store vínbúð [veanbuhth]

liter lítri [leatri]

little lítill [leatiddl]

live v lifa [lifa] **~ music** lifandi tónlist [lifandi tohnlist]

liver (body part) lifur [lifur]

loafers inniskór [inniskohr]

local n (person) heimamaður [heymamathur]

lock v læsa [laysa] **~** n lás [lous]

locker skápur [skoupur]

log off v (computer) útskráning [uhtskrou-neang]

log on (computer) innskráning [innskrou-neang]

long adj langur [loungur] **--sighted** [BE] fjarsýnn [fjarseadn] **--sleeved** langerma [langerma]

look v líta [leata] **~ for something** leita að einhverju [leyta ath eynhverju]

loose (fit) laus [luys]

lose v (something) týna [teana]

lost týnt [teant] **~-and-found** óskilamunir [ohskilamunir]

lotion áburður [ouburthur]

louder hærra [hayrra]

love v (someone) elska [elska] **~** n ást [oust]

low adj lágur [loughur]

luggage farangur [faroungur] **~ cart** farangurskerra [faroun-gurskerra] **~ locker** farangursskápur [faroungursskoupur] **~ ticket** farangursmiði [faroungursmithi]

lunch n hádegismatur [houdeghismatur]

lung lunga [loungu]

luxury car lúxusbifreið [luhxusbifreyth]

M

machine washable má setja í þvottavél [mou setja ea thvottavyel]

magazine tímarit [teamarit]

magnificent stórkostlegt [stohrkostleght]

mail v senda póst [senda pohst] **~** n póstur [pohstur] **~box** pósthólf [pohsthohlf]

main attraction helsta skoðunarstaðir [helstu skothunarstathir]

main course helstu leiðir [helstu leythir]

mall verslunarmiðstöð [verslunarmithstuhth]

man (adult male) maður [mathur]

manager framkvæm-dastjóri [framkvaym-dastjohri]

manicure n handsnyrting [handsnyrteang]

manual car beinskiptur bíll [beynskiftur beaddl]

map n landakort [landakort] **~** n (town) bæjarkort [bayjarkort]

market n markaður [markathur]

married giftur [giftur]

marry giftast [giftast]

mass n (church service) messa [messa]

massage n nudd [nudd]

match n jafningi [jabneangi]

meal máltíð [moulteath]

measure v (someone) mæla [mayla]

measuring cup mæliglas [mayliglas]

measuring spoon mæliskeið [mayliskeyth]

mechanic n vélvirki [vyelvirki]

medication (drugs) lyfjameðferð [lyfjameth-ferth]

medicine lyf [lif]

medium (steak) miðlungs [mithloongs]

meet v hitta [hitta]

meeting n (business) fundur [fundur] **~ room** fundarherbergi [fundarherbergi]

membership card aðildarskírteini [athildarskearteyni]

memorial (place) minnisvarði [minnisvarthi]

memory card minniskort [minniskort]

mend v (clothes) bæta [bayta]

menstrual cramps tíðakrampi [teathakrampi]

menu (restaurant) matseðill [matsethiddl]

message skilaboð [skilaboth]

meter n (parking) mælir [maylir] **~** n (measure) metri [metri]

microwave n örbylgjuofn [uhrbylgjuobn]

midday [BE] miðdegi [mithdeghi]

midnight miðnætti [mithnaytti]

mileage ending [endeang]

mini-bar mínibar [meaneabar]

minute mínúta [meanuhta]

missing (not there) vantar [vantar]

mistake n mistök [mistuhk]

mobile home húsbíll [huhsbeaddl]

mobile phone [BE] farsími [farseami]

mobility hreyfanleiki [hreyfanleyki]

monastery klaustur [kluystur]

money peningar [peneangar]

month mánuður [mounuthur]

mop n moppa [moppa]

moped létt bifhjól [lyett bífhjóhl]
more meira [meyra]
morning n morgunn [morgunn]
mosque moska [moska]
mother n móðir [mohthir]
motion sickness ferðaveiki [ferthaveyki]
motor n mótor [mohtor]
~ **boat** mótorbátur [mohtorboutur] **~cycle** mótorhjól [mohtorhjohl] **~way** (BE) hraðbraut [hrathbruyt]
mountain fjall [fjaddl]
~ **bike** fjallahjól [fjaddlahjohl]
mousse (hair) froða [frotha]
mouth n munnur [munnur]
movie bíómynd [beeohmynd] **~ theater** bíó [beeoh]
mug n ræna [rayna]
multiple-trip ticket fjölnota miði [fjuhlnota mithi]
muscle n vöðvi [vuhthvi]
museum safn [sabn]
music tónlist [tohnlist] **~ store** tónlistarverslun [tohnlistarverslun]

N

nail file naglaþjöl [naglathjuhl]
nail salon naglasnyrtistofa [naglasnyrtistofa]
name n nafn [nabn]
napkin servíetta [serveaetta]
nappy (BE) bleyja [bleyja]
nationality þjóðerni [thjohtherdni]
nature preserve náttúruverndarsvæði [nouttuhruverndarsvaythi]
nausea ógleði [ohglethi]
nauseous óglatt [ohglatt]
near nálægt [noulaygt] **~-sighted** nærsýnn [nayrseadn]

nearby nálægt [noulaygt]
neck n háls [houls]
necklace hálsmen [houlsmen]
need v þurfa [thurfa]
newspaper dagblað [daghblath]
newsstand blaðsölustaður [blathsuhlustathur]
next adj næstur [naystur]
nice góður [gohthur]
night nótt [nohtt] **~club** næturklúbbur [nayturkloobbur]
no nei [ney] **~ (not any)** enginn [eynginn]
non-alcoholic án alkóhóls [oun alkohhohls]
non-smoking adj reyklaus [reykluys]
noon n hádegi [houdeghi]
north n norður [northur]
nose nef [nef]
note n [BE] (money) seðill [sethiddl]
nothing ekkert [eckert]
notify v tilkynna [tilkinna]
novice n nýliði [nealithi]
now núna [nuhna]
number n númer [nuhmer]
nurse n hjúkrunarfræðingur [hjuhkrunarfraytheangur]

O

office skrifstofa [skrifstofa] **~ hours** skrifstofutími [skrifstofuteami]
off-licence [BE] vínbúð [veanbuhth]
oil n olía [oleaa]
OK í lagi [ea laghi]
old adj gamall [gamaddl]
on the corner á horninu [ou hordninu]
once (one time) einu sinni [eynu sinni]
one einn [eydn] **(counting)** einn [eydn] **~-day (ticket)** einsdagsmiði [eynsdaghsmithi] **~-way ticket (airline)** farmiði

aðra leiðina [farmithi athra leythina] **~-way street** einstefnugata [eynstebnugata]
only aðeins [atheyns]
open v opna [opna] ~ adj opinn [opinn]
opera ópera [ohpera] **~ house** óperuhús [ohperohoos]
opposite n andstæða [andstaytha]
optician augnlæknir [uygnlayknir]
orange adj (color) appelsínugulur [appelseanugulur]
orchestra hljómsveit [hljohmsveyt]
order n (restaurant) pöntun [puhntun]
outdoor pool útisundlaug [uhtisundluyg]
outside prep utan við [utan vith]
over prep (direction) ofan við [ofan vith] **~done (meat)** ofeldaður [ofeldathur] **~heat** v (car) ofhitaður [ofhitathur] **~look** n (scenic place) yfirsýn [yfirsean] **~night** yfir nótt [yfir nohtt] **~-the-counter (medication)** yfir borðið [ifir borthith]
oxygen treatment súrefnismeðferð [suhrebnismethferth]

P

p.m. eftir hádegi [eftir houdeghi]
pacifier snuð [snuth]
pack v pakka [packa]
package n pakki [packi]
pad [BE] púði [puhthi]
paddling pool [BE] vaðtjörn [vathtjuhrdn]
pain sársauki [soursuyki]
pajamas náttföt [nouttfuht]
palace höll [huhddl]

pants buxur [buxur]
pantyhose sokkabuxur [sockabuxur]
paper n (material) pappír [pappear] **~ towel** pappírsþurrka [pappearsthurrka]
paracetamol [BE] parasetamól [parasetamohl]
park v leggja [leggja] ~ n garður [garthur] **~ing garage** bílastæðahús [bealastaythahoos] **~ing lot** bílastæði [bealastaythi] **~ing meter** stöðumælir [stuhthumaylir]
parliament building þinghús [theanghuhs]
part (for car) hlutur [hlutur] **~-time** adj í hlutastarfi [ea hlutastarfi]
pass through v (travel) fara í gegnum [fara ea gegnum]
passenger farþegi [fartheghi]
passport vegabréf [veghabref] **~ control** vegabréfsskoðun [veghabryefsskothun]
password lykilorð [likilorth]
pastry shop bakarí [bakarea]
patch v (clothing) bjatla [bjatla]
path slóð [slohth]
pay v borga [borga] **~phone** almenningssími [almenneangsseami]
peak n (of a mountain) tindur [tindur]
pearl n perla [perla]
pedestrian n vegfarandi [veghfarandi]
pediatrician barnalæknir [bardnalayknir]
pedicure n fótsnyrting [fohtsnirteang]
pen n penni [penni]
penicillin pensillín

[pensillean]

penis getnaðarlimur [getnatharlimur]

per á [ou] ~ **day** á dag [ou dagh] ~ **hour** á klukkustund [ou kluckoustund] ~ **night** á nótt [ou nohtt] ~ **week** á viku [ou viku]

perfume n ilmvatn [ilmvatn]

period (menstrual) tíðir [teathir] ~ **(of time)** tímabil [teamabil]

permit v leyfa [leyfa]

petrol [BE] bensín [bensean] ~ **station** [BE] bensínstöð [benseanstuhth]

pewter blikk [blick]

pharmacy apótek [apohtek]

phone n hringja [hreangja] ~ n sími [seami] ~ **call** simtal [seamtal] ~ **card** símakort [seamakort] ~ **number** símanúmer [seamanoomper]

photo ljósmynd [ljohsmind] ~**copy** ljósrit [ljohsrit] ~**graphy** ljósmyndun [ljohsmyndun]

pick up v **(person)** sækja [saykja]

picnic area nestisferðasvæði [nestisferthasvaythi]

piece n stykki [sticki]

Pill (birth control) pilla [pilla]

pillow n koddi [koddi]

pink adj bleikur [bleykur]

piste [BE] braut [bruyt] ~ **map** n brautakort [bruytakort]

pizzeria pitsustaður [peatsustathur]

place v **(a bet)** setja [setja]

plane n flugvél [flughvyel]

plastic wrap plastumbúðir [plastumbuhthir]

plate n diskur [diskur]

platform [BE] **(train)** pallur [paddlur]

platinum n platína [plateana]

play v spila [spila] ~ n **(theatre)** leikrit [leikrit] ~**ground** leikvöllur [leykvuhddlur] ~**pen** leikgrind [leykgrind]

please adv vinsamlegast [vinsamleghast]

pleasure n ánægja [ounayghja]

plunger drullusokkur [druddlusockur]

plus size n aukastærð [uykastayrth]

pocket n vasi [vasi]

poison n eitur [eytur]

poles (skiing) stöng [stuhng]

police lögregla [luhgregla] ~ **report** lögregluskýrsla [luhgreghluskearsla] ~ **station** lögreglustöð [luhgreghlustuhth]

pond n tjörn [tjuhrdn]

pool n laug [luygh]

pop music popptónlist [popptohnlist]

portion n skammtur [skammtur]

post n [BE] póstur [pohstur] ~ **office** pósthús [pohsthoos] ~**box** [BE] pósthólf [pohsthohlf] ~**card** póstkort [pohstkort]

pot n pottur [pottur]

pottery leirkeragerð [leyrkeragerth]

pound n (weight) pund [pund] ~ **(British sterling)** pund [pund]

pregnant barnshafandi [bardnshafandi]

prescribe (medication) ávísa [ouveasa]

prescription lyfseðill [lifsethiddl]

press v **(clothing)** pressa [pressa]

price n verð [verth]

print v prenta [prenta] ~ n

prent [prent]

problem vandamál [vandamoul]

produce n afurð [afurth] ~ **store** afurðaverslun [afurthaverslun]

prohibit banna [banna]

pronounce bera fram [bera fram]

Protestant Mótmælandi [Mohtmaylandi]

public adj opinber [opinber]

pull v draga [dragha]

purple adj fjólublár [fjohlublour]

purse n budda [budda]

push v ýta [eata] ~**chair** [BE] barnakerra [bardnakerra]

Q

quality n gæði [gaythi]

question n spurning [spurdneang]

quiet adj rólegur [rohleghur]

R

racetrack kappakstursbraut [kappakstursbruyt]

racket n **(sports)** tennisspaði [tennisspathi]

railway station [BE] lestarstöð [lestarstuhth]

rain n rigning [rigneang] ~**coat** regnkápa [regnkoupa] ~**forest** regnskógur [regnskohghur] ~**y** votviðrasamur [votvithrasamur]

rap n (music) rapp [rapp]

rape v nauðga [nuythga] ~ n nauðgun [nuythgun]

rare adj sjaldgæfur [sjaldgayfur]

rash n útbrot [uhtbrot]

ravine gil [gil]

razor blade rakvélablað [rakvyelablath]

reach v ná [nou]

ready tilbúinn [tilbuhinn]

real adj raunverulegur

[ruynveruleghur]

receipt n kvittun [kvittun]

receive v fá [fou]

reception (hotel) móttaka [mohttaka]

recharge v endurhlaða [endurhlatha]

recommend mæla með [mayla meth]

recommendation meðmæli [methmayli]

recycling endurvinnsla [endurvinnsla]

red adj rauður [ruythur]

refrigerator ísskápur [easskoupur]

region svæði [svaythi]

registered mail ábyrgðarpóstur [oubyrghtharpohstur]

regular n **(fuel)** venjulegur [venjuleghur]

relationship samband [samband]

rent n leigja [leyghja] ~ n leiga [leygha]

rental car bílaleigubíll [bealaleyghubeaddl]

repair v gera við [gera vith]

repeat v endurtaka [endurtaka]

reservation pöntun [puhntun] ~ **desk** pantanaborð [pantanaborth]

reserve v **(hotel)** panta [panta]

restaurant veitingastaður [veyteangastathur]

restroom salerni [salerdni]

retired adj **(from work)** eftirlaunaþegi [eftirluynatheghi]

return v **(something)** skila [skila] ~ n [BE] **(trip)** heimkoma [heymkoma]

reverse v (the charges) [BE] bakfæra [bakfayra]

rib n **(body part)** rifbein [rifbeyn]

right adj, adv **(direction)** hægri [hayghri] ~ **of way** hægri réttur

[hayghri ryettur]

ring n hringur [hreangur]

river á [ou]

road map vegakort [vegakort]

rob v ræna [rayna]

robbed rændur [rayndur]

romantic adj rómantískur [rohmanteaskur]

room n herbergi [herbergi]
~ **key** herbergislykill [herbergislykiddl] ~ **service** herbergisþjónusta [herbergisthjohnusta]

round trip hringferð [hreangferth]

route n leið [leyth]

rowboat árabátur [ouraboutur]

rubbing alcohol sótthreinsandi vökvi [sohtthreynsandi vuhkvi]

rubbish n [BE] rusl [rusl]
~ **bag** [BE] ruslapoki [ruslapoki]

rugby n ruðningur [ruthneangur]

ruin n rúst [ruhst]

rush v þjóta [thjohta]

S

sad dapur [dapur]

safe (protected) öruggur [uhruggur] ~ n **(thing)** öruggt [uhruggt]

sales tax söluskattur [suhluskattur]

same adj eins [eyns]

sandals sandalar [sandalar]

sanitary napkin dömubindi [duhmubindi]

sauna gufubað [gufubath]

sauté v snöggsteikja [snuhggsteykja]

save v **(computer)** vista [vista]

savings (account) sparnaður [spardnathur]

scanner skanni [skanni]

scarf hálsklútur [houlskluhtur]

schedule v áætla [ouaytla]

~ áætlun [ouaytlun]

school n skóli [skohli]

science vísindi [veasindi]

scissors skæri [skayri]

sea sjór [sjohr]

seat n sæti [sayti]

security öryggi [uhryggi]

see v sjá [sjou]

self-service n sjálfsþjónusta [sjoulfsthjoh-nusta]

sell v selja [selja]

seminar námskeið [noumskeyth]

send v senda [senda]

senior citizen eldri borgari [eldri borgari]

separated (person) skilinn [skilinn]

serious alvarlegur [alvarleghur]

service (in a restaurant) þjónusta [thjohnusta]

sexually transmitted disease (STD) kynsjúkdómur [kynsjuhkdohmur]

shampoo n sjampó [sjampoh]

sharp adj beittur [beyttur]

shaving cream raksápa [raksoupa]

sheet n **(bed)** lak [lak]

ship v skip [skip]

shirt skyrta [skirta]

shoe store skóbúð [skohbuhth]

shoe skór [skohr]

shop v verslan [versla] ~ n verslun [verslun]

shopping n innkaup [innkuyp] ~ **area** verslunarsvæði [verslunarsvaythi] ~ **centre** [BE] verslunarmiðstöð [verslunarmithstuhth] ~ **mall** verslunarmiðstöð [verslunarmithstuhth]

short stutt [stutt]

~~**sleeved** stutterma [stutterma]

shorts stuttbuxur [stuttbuxur]

short-sighted [BE]

nærsýnn [nayrseadn]

shoulder n öxl [uhxl]

show v sýna [seana]

shower (bath) sturta [sturta]

shrine helgidómur [helgidohmur]

sick adj veikur [veykur]

side n hlið [hlith] ~ **dish** meðlæti [methlayti]
~ **effect** aukaverkun [uykaverkun] ~ **order** meðlætispöntun [methlaytispuhntun]

sightseeing skoðunarferðir [skothunarferthir]
~ **tour** skoðunarferð [skothunarferth]

sign v **(document)** undirrita [undirrita]

silk silki [silki]

silver n silfur [silfur]

single adj **(person)** einhleypur [eynhleypur]
~ **bed** eitt rúm [eytt room] ~ **print** einrit [eynrit] ~ **room** eitt herbergi [eytt herbergi]

sink n vaskur [vaskur]

sister systir [sistir]

sit v sitja [sitja]

size n stærð [stayrth]

ski v skíða [skeatha] ~ **lift** skíðalyfta [skeathalyfta]

skin n húð [huhth]

skirt n pils [pils]

sleep v sofa [sofa]
~**er car** svefnvagn [svebnvagn] ~**ing bag** svefnpoki [svebnpoki] ~**ing car** [BE] svefnvagn [svebnvagn]

slice n sneið [sneyth]

slippers inniskór [in-niskohr]

slower hægari [hayghari]

slowly hægt [hayght]

small lítill [leatiddl]

smoke v reykja [reykja]

smoking (area) reykingasvæði [reykeangasvaythi]

snack bar snarl [snarl]

sneakers íþróttaskór [eathrohttaskohr]

snowboard n snjóbretti [snjohbretti]

snowshoe n snjóþrúga [snjohthruhgha]

snowy snævi þakinn [snayvi thakinn]

soap n sápa [soupa]

soccer knattspyrna [knattspyrdna]

sock sokkur [sockur]

some (with singular nouns) einhver [eyn-hver] ~ **(with plural nouns)** einhverjir [eynhverjir]

soother [BE] snudda [snudda]

sore throat hálsbólga [houlsbohlga]

south n suður [suthur]

souvenir n minjagripur [minjagripur] ~ **store** minjagripaverslun [minjagripaverslun]

spa heilsulind [heylsulind]

spatula spaði [spathi]

speak v tala [tala]

specialist (doctor) sérfræðingur [syerfray-theangur]

specimen sýnishorn [seanishordn]

speeding hraðakstur [hrathakstur]

spell v stafa [stafa]

spicy kryddaður [kriddathur] ~ **(not bland)** hressilegur [hressileghur]

spine (body part) hryggur [hriggur]

spoon n skeið [skeyth]

sports íþróttir [eathrohttir]
~ **massage** íþróttanudd [eathrohttanudd]

sprain n togna [toggna]

stadium völlur [vuhddlur]

stairs stigi [stighi]

stamp n **(ticket)** stimpill [stimpiddl] ~ n **(postage)** frímerki

[freamerki]
start v byrja [birja]
starter [BE] forrettur [forryettur]
station n (stop) stöð [stuhth] **bus** ~ strætostöð [straytohstuhth]
gas ~ bensinstöð [benseanstuhth] **petrol** ~ [BE] bensinstöð [benseanstuhth] **subway** ~ neðanjarðarlestarstöð [nethanjartharlestarstuhth] **train** ~ lestarstöð [lestarstuhth]
statue stytta [stitta]
steakhouse steikhús [steykhuhs]
steal v stela [stela]
steep adj bratt [bratt]
sterling silver ekta silfur [ekta silfur]
sting n stingur [steangur]
stolen stolinn [stolinn]
stomach magi [maghi] **~ache** magaverkur [maghaverkur]
stool (bowel movement) hægðir [hayghthir]
stop v (bus) stöðva [stuhthva] ~ n (transportation) stoppistöð [stoppistuhth]
store directory (mall) verslanaskrá [verslanaskrou]
storey [BE] hæð [hayth]
stove n eldavél [eldavyel]
straight adv (direction) beint [bpynt]
strange undarlegt [undarlegt]
stream n lækur [laykur]
stroller (baby) barnakerra [bardnakerra]
student (university) háskólanemi [houskohlanemi] ~ (school) nemandi [nemandi]
study n rannsókn [rannsohkn] ~ing n lærir [layrir]

stuffed uppstoppaður [uppstoppathur]
stunning glæsilegur [ghlaysileghur]
subtitle n texti [texti] ...... ~ station textastöð [textastuhth]
suit n föt [fuht] ~case ferðataska [ferthataska]
sun n sól [sohl] ~block sólarvörn [sohlaruhrn] ~burn sólbruni [sohlbruni] ~glasses sólgleraugu [sohlgleruyghu] ~ny sólríkt [sohlreakt] ~screen sólhlíf [sohlhlaf] ~stroke sólstingur [sohlsteangur]
super v (fuel) súper [suhper] ~market stórmarkaður [stohrmarkathur]
surfboard brimbretti [brimbretti]
surgical spirit [BE] etanól [etanohl]
swallow v gleypa [gleypa]
sweater peysa [peysa]
sweatshirt peysa [peysa]
sweet n [BE] sælgæti [saylgayti] ~ adj (taste) sætur [saytur]
swelling bólga [bohlga]
swim v synda [sinda] ~suit sundföt [sundfuht]
symbol (keyboard) tákn [toukn]
synagogue bænahús [baynahuhs]

T
table n borð [borth]
tablet (medicine) tafla [tafla]
take v taka [taka]
tampon n tíðatappi [teathatappi]
taste n (test) bragð [braghth]
taxi n leigubíll [leyghubeaddl]
team n lið [lith]

teaspoon teskeið [teskeyth]
telephone n sími [seami]
temple (religious) musteri [musteri]
temporary tímabundið [teamabundith]
tennis tennis [tennis]
tent n tjald [tjald] ~peg tjaldhæll [tjaldhayddl] ~ pole tjaldsúla [tjaldsoola]
terminal n (airport) flugstöð [flughstuhth]
terrible hræðilegur [hraythileghur]
text v (send a message) texta [texta] ~ n texti [texti]
thank v þakka [thacka] ~ you þakka þér fyrir [thacka thyer fyrir]
the n[A
theater leikhús [leykhuhs]
theft þjófnaður [thjohbnathur]
there þar [thar]
thief þjófur [thjohfur]
thigh læri [layri]
thirsty þyrstur [thyrstur]
this þetta [thetta]
throat háls [houls]
thunderstorm þrumuveður [thrumuvethur]
ticket n miði [mithi] ~ office miðasala [mithasala]
tie n (clothing) hálsbindi [houlsbindi]
tight (fit) þröngur [thruhngur]
tights [BE] sokkabuxur [sockabuxur]
time tími [teami] ~table [BE] (transportation) tímatafla [teamatafla]
tire n hjólbarði [hjohlbarthi]
tired þreyttur [threyttur]
tissue pappírsþurrka [pappearsthurrka]
tobacconist tóbakssali [tohbakssali]
today adv í dag [ea dagh]

toe n tá [tou]
toenail tánögl [tounuhgl]
toilet [BE] salerni [salerdni] ~ paper salernispappír [salerdnispappear]
tomorrow adv á morgun [ou morgun]
tongue n tunga [toonga]
tonight í kvöld [ea kvuhld]
to (direction) til [til]
tooth tönn [tuhnn]
toothpaste tannkrem [tannkrem]
total n (amount) samtals [samtals]
tough adj (food) seigur [seyghur]
tour n ferðalag [ferthalagh]
tourist ferðamaður [ferthamathur] ~ information office ferðamannaupplýsingar [ferthamannuypplea-seangar]
tow truck dráttarbíll [drouttarbeaddl]
towel n handklæði [handklaythi]
tower n turn [turdn]
town bær [bayr] ~ hall ráðhús [routhhoos] ~ map bæjarkort [bayjarkort] ~ square bæjartorg [bayjartorg]
toy leikfang [leykfoung] ~ store leikfangaverslun [leykfoungaverslun]
track n (train) spor [spor]
traditional hefðbundinn [hefthbundinn]
traffic light umferðarljós [umfertharljohs]
trail n (ski) slóð [slohth] ~ map gönguleiðakort [guhnguleythakort]
trailer (car) tengivagn [teyngivagn]
train n lest [lest] ~ station lestarstöð [lestarstuhth]
transfer v (change trains[flights)

skipta um [skifta um] ~ **(money)** millifæra [middlifayra]

translate þýða [theatha]

trash n rusl [rusl]

travel n ferðalag [ferthalagh]
– **agency** ferðaskrifstofa [ferthaskrifstofa] ~ **sickness** ferðaveiki [ferthaveyki] ~**ers check [cheque** BE] ferðatékki [ferthatyecki]

tree tré [trye]

trim (hair) v snyrta [snirta]

trip n ferð [ferth]

trolley [BE**] (grocery store)** kerra [kerra] ~ **[**BE**] (luggage)** farangurskerra [faroungurskerra]

trousers [BE**]** buxur [buxur]

T-shirt stuttermabolur [stuttermabolur]

tumble dry þurrka [thurrka]

turn off v **(device)** slökkva á [sluhckva ou]

turn on v **(device)** kveikja á [kveykja ou]

TV sjónvarp [sjohnvarp]

tyre [BE**]** hjólbarði [hjohlbarthi]

U

ugly ljótur [ljohtur]

umbrella regnhlíf [regnhleaf]

unbranded medication [BE**]** övörumerkt lyf [ohvuhrumerkt lyf]

unconscious (faint) meðvitundarlaus [methvitundarluys]

underdone of lítið eldaður [of leatith eldathur]

underground n [BE] neðanjarðar [nethanjarthar] ~ **station [**BE**]** neðanjarðarstöð [nethanjartharstuhth]

underpants [BE**]** nærbuxur [nayrbuxur]

understand v skilja [skilja]

underwear nærföt [nayrfuht]

United Kingdom (U.K.) Bretland [Bretland]

United States (U.S.) Bandaríkin [Bandareakin]

university háskóli [houskohli]

unleaded (gas) blýlaust [blealuyst]

upset stomach órólegur í maganum [ohrohleghur ea maghanum]

urgent áríðandi [oureathandi]

urine þvag [thvagh]

use v nota [nota]

username notandafn [notandanbn]

utensil áhald [ouhald]

V

vacancy (room) laust [luyst]

vacation frí [frea]

vaccination bólusetning [bohlusetneang]

vacuum cleaner ryksuga [riksugha]

vaginal infection sýking í leggöngum [seakeangh ea leghghuhnghum]

valid gildur [gildur]

valley dalur [dalur]

valuable n dýrmætur [dearmaytur]

value n gildi [gildi]

van sendibíll [sendibeaddl]

VAT [BE**]** virðisaukaskattur [virthisuykaskattur]

vegan n vegan [vegan] ~ adj vegan [vegan]

vegetarian n grænmetis [graynmetis] ~ adj grænmetisæta [graynmetisayta]

vehicle registration skráning ökutækis [skrouneang uhkutaykis]

viewpoint (scenic) [BE] útsýnisstaður [uhtseanisstathur]

village þorp [thorp]

vineyard vínekra [veanekra]

visa vegabréfsáritun [veghabreyfsouritun]

visit v heimsókn [heymsohkn] ~**ing hours** heimsóknartími [heymsohknarteami]

visually impaired sjónskertur [sjohnskertur]

vitamin vítamín [veatamean]

V-neck v-hálsmál [v-houlsmoul]

volleyball game blak [blak]

vomit v kasta upp [kasta upp] ~**ing** kastar upp [kastar upp]

W

wait v bíða [beatha] ~ n bið [bith]

waiter þjónn [thjohdn]

waiting room biðstofa [bithstofa]

waitress gengilbeina [geyngilbeyna]

wake v vekja [vekja] ~**-up call** vakning [vakneang]

walk v ganga [gounga] ~ n göngutúr [guhngutoor] ~**ing route** gönguleið [guhnguleyth]

wallet veski [veski]

war memorial stríðsminnisvarði [streathsminnisvarthi]

warm v (something) hita [hita] ~ adj **(temperature)** heitt [heytt]

washing machine þvottavél [thvottavyel]

watch v horfa [horfa]

waterfall foss [foss]

wax v **(hair)** vax [vax]

weather n veður [vethur]

week vika [vika] ~**end** helgi [helgi]

weekly vikulega [vikulegha]

welcome adj velkominn [velkominn] **you're ~** gjörðu svo vel [gjuhrthu svo vel]

west n vestur [vestur]

what hvað [hvath]

wheelchair hjólastóll [hjohlastohddl] ~ **ramp** hjólastólarampur [hjohlastohlarampur]

when adv (at what time) hvenær [hvenayr]

where hvar [hvar]

white adj hvítur [hveatur] ~ **gold** hvítagull [hveatuguddl]

who (question) hver [hver]

widowed ekkja [eckja]

wife eiginkona [eyghinkona]

window gluggi [gluggi] ~ **case** gluggakarmur [gluggakarmur]

wine list vínlisti [veanlisti]

wireless þráðlaus [throuthluys] ~ **phone** þráðlaus sími [throuthluys seami]

with með [meth]

withdraw v (money) taka út [taka uht] ~**al (bank)** úttekt [oottekt]

without án [oun]

woman kona [kona]

wool ull [uddl]

work v vinna [vinna]

wrap v pakka inn [packa inn]

wrist úlnliður [uhlnlithur]

write v skrifa [skrifa]

Y

year ár [our]

yellow adj gulur [gulur]

yes já [ou]

yesterday adv í gær [ea gayr]

young adj ungur [oongur]

youth hostel farfuglaheimili [farfuglaheymili]

Z

zoo dýragarður [dearagarthur]

ICELANDIC - ENGLISH

A

aðeins [atheyns] only

aðgangseyrir [athgoungseyrir] admission (price), cover charge

aðgangur [athgoungur] access n

aðildarskirteini [athildarskearteyni] membership card

aðlaðandi [athlathandi] attractive

afmælisdagur [afmaylisdaghur] birthday

afsaka [afsaka] excuse v

afsláttur [afslouttur] discount n

aftengja [afteyngja] disconnect (computer)

afurð [afurth] produce n

afurðaverslun [afurthaverslun] produce store

aka [aka] drive v

án alkóhóls [oun alkohhohls] non alcoholic

aldur [aldur] age n

afgangur [afgoungur] change n (money)

almennt farrými [almennt farreami] economy class

almenningssími [almenneangsseami] pay phone

alvarlegur [alvarleghur] serious

alþjóðlegur [althjohthleghur] international

alþjóðlegt nemendaskirteini international student card [althjohthleght nemendaskearteyni]

amma og afi [amma ogh afi] grandparents

anda [anda] breathe

andlit [andlit] face n

andlitssnyrting [andlitssnyrteanj] facial n

andstæða [andstaytha] opposite n

apótek [apohtek] pharmacy

apótekari [apohtekari] chemist [BE]

appelsínugulur [appelseanugulur] orange adj [color]

armband [armband] bracelet

asískur [aseaskur] Asian adj

aspirin [aspiran] aspirin

athuga [athugha] check (on something) n

athugun [athughun] payment

auðkenni [uythkenni] identification

auðvelt [uythvelt] easy

auga [uygha] eye

augabrúnavax [uyghabruhnavax] eyebrow wax

augnlinsa [augnlinsa] contact lens

augnlinsulausn [uygnlinsuluysn] contact lens solution

augnlæknir [uygnlayknir] optician

auka [uyka] extra adj

aukastærð [uykastayrth] plus size

aukaverkun [uykaverkun] side effect

austur [uystur] east n

aðgangskort [athgoungskort] key card

aðgangur fyrir fatlaða [athgoungur fyrir fatlatha] disabled / handicapped accessible

á [ou] per

á dag [ou dagh] per day

á klukkustund [ou kluccustund] per hour

á nótt [ou nohtt] per night

á viku [ou viku] per week

á [ou] river

á horninu [ou hordninu] on the corner

á meðan [ou methan] during

á morgun [ou morgun] tomorrow adv

áburður [ouburthur] lotion

ábyrgðarpóstur [oubyrghtharpohstur] registered mail

áður [outhur] earlier

áhald [ouhald] utensil

áhugavert [ouhughavert] interesting

áletra [ouletra] engrave

álpappír [oulpappear] aluminum foil

án [oun] without

ánægja [ounayghja] pleasure n

ár [our] year

árabátur [ouraboutur] rowboat

áríðandi [oureathandi] urgent

ást [oust] love n

ástand [oustand] condition (medical)

Ástralía [Oustraleaa] Australia

ástralskur [oustralskur] Australian adj

átt [outt] direction

ávísa [ouveasa] prescribe (medication)

ávísanareikningur [ouveasanareykneangur] current account [BE]

áætla [ouaytla] schedule v

áætlun [ouaytlun] schedule n

B

baðherbergi [bathherbergi] bathroom

bak [bak] back (body part)

bakverkur [bakverkur] backache

bakpoki [bakpoki] backpack

baka [baka] bake v

bakarí [bakarea] bakery, pastry shop pastry shop

bakfæra [bakfayra] reverse v (the charges) [BE]

ballett [ballett] ballet

Bandaríkin [Bandareakin] United States (U.S.)

bandarískur [bandareaskur] American adj

banki [banki] bank n

banna [banna] prohibit

bar [bar] bar (place)

barn [bardn] baby

barnakerra [bardnakerra] pushchair [BE]

barnfóstra [bardnfohstra] babysitter

barn [bardn] child

barnastóll [bardnastohddl] child's seat

barnabarn [bardnabardn] grandchild

barnakerra [bardnakerra] stroller (baby)

barnalæknir [bardnalayknir] pediatrician

barnamatseðill [bardnamatsethill] children's menu

barnarúm [bardnaroom] crib

barnaskammtur [bardnaskammtur] children's portion

barnasundlaug [bardnasundluygh] kiddie pool

barnshafandi [bardnshafandi] pregnant

bátur [boutur] boat n

bein [beyn] bone n

bein lína [beyn leana] extension (phone)

beinskiptur bíll [beynskiftur beaddl] manual car

beint [beynt] straight adv (direction)

beittur [beyttur] sharp adj

belti [belti] belt

bensín [bensean] gas (car), petrol

bensínstöð [benseanstuhht] gas station, petrol station

bera fram [bera fram] pronounce

bestur [bestur] best adj

best fyrir [best fyrir] best before

betri [betri] better

biðstofa [bithstofa] waiting room

bikiní [bikinea] bikini

bilun [bilun] breakdown (car)

bíða [beatha] wait v

bíð [bith] wait n

bílaleigubíll [bealaleyghubeaddl] rental car

bílaleigubifreið [bealaleyghubifreyth] hire **car** [BE]

bílaleiga [bealaleygha] car hire, car rental

bíll [beall] car

bílastæði [bealastaythi] car park, parking lot

bílastæðahús [bealastaythahoos] parking garage

bílsæti [bealsayti] car seat

bílskúr [bealskuhr] garage n [parking]

bíómynd [beaohmynd] movie

bíó [beaoh] movie theater

bjarg [bjarg] cliff

björgunarvesti [bjuhrgunarvesti] life jacket

blaðra [blathra] bladder

blaðsölustaður [blathsuhlustathur] newsstand

blak [blak] volleyball game

blanda [blanda] bland, formula (baby)

blandari [blandari] blender

blár [blour] blue adj

bleikur [bleykur] pink adj

bless [bless] bye, goodbye

bleyja [bleyja] diaper,

nappy [BE] **nappy** [BE]

blikk [blick] pewter

blóð [blohth] blood

blóðþrýstingur [blohth-threasteangur] blood pressure

blóðlaus [blohthluys] anemic

blóm [blohm] flower n

blómabúð [blohmabuhth] florist

blúndur [bluhndur] lace n (fabric)

blússa [bloossa] blouse

blýlaust [blealuyst] unleaded (gas)

blæða [blaytha] bleed

bolli [bolli] cup n

borð [borth] table n

borða [bortha] eat v

borðsalur [borthsalur] dining room

borga [borga] pay v

botnlangi [botnloungi] appendix (body part)

bók [bohk] book n

bókabúð [bohkabooth] book store

bókasafn [bohkasabn] library

bólga [bohlga] swelling

bólusetning [bohlusetneang] vaccination

bómull [bohmull] cotton

bóndabær [bohndabayr] farm

bragð [braghth] taste v (test)

bratt [bratt] steep adj

braut [bruyt] piste [BE]

brautakort [bruytakort] piste map [BE]

bremsa [bremsa] brake (car)

brenna [brenna] burn v

breskur [breskur] British adj

Bretland [Bretland] United Kingdom (UK)

breyta [breyta] alter v

bréf [bryef] letter n

brimbretti [brimbretti] surfboard

bringa [breanga] chest

(body part)

brjóstverkur [brjohst-verkur] chest pain

brjóst [brjohst] breast

brjóstagjöf [brjohstagjuhf] breastfeed

brjóstahaldari [brjohsta-haldari] bra

brjóta [brjohta] break v (bone)

brotinn [brotinn] broken

brotið [brotith] broken bone

brottfararspjald [brottfara-rspjald] boarding pass

brottför [brottfur] departure (plane)

bróðir [brohthir] bother v, brother brother

brú [broo] bridge

brúða [bruhtha] doll n

brúnn [broonn] brown adj

budda [budda] purse n

buxur [buxur] pants, trousers [BE]

bygging [biggeang] building

byrja [birja] begin, start v

byrjandi [birjandi] beginner

bænahús [baynahuhs] synagogue

bær [bayr] town

bæjarkort [bayjarkort] town map

bæjartorg [bayjartorg] town square

bæta [bayta] mend v (clothes)

C

celsíus [celseaus] Celsius

D

dagblað [daghblath] newspaper

dagsetning [daghsetne-angh] date n (calendar)

dagur [daghur] day

dalur [dalur] valley

dansa [dansa] dance v

dansklúbbur [danskloob-bur] dance club

dans [dans] dancing

dapur [dapur] sad

debetkort [debetkort] debit card

deildaskipt verslun [deyldaskift verslun] department store

demantur [demantur] diamond

denim [deneam] denim

deyfing [deyfeang] anesthesia

dimmt [dimmt] dark adj

diskar [diskar] dishes (kitchen)

diskur [diskur] plate n

disel [deasel] diesel

djass [djass] jazz n

djassklúbbur [djasskloob-bur] jazz club

djúpur [djuhpur] deep adj

dollari [dollari] dollars

dómkirkja [dohmkirkja] cathedral

dósahnífur [dohsahneafur] can opener

draga [draga] extract v (tooth)

draga [dragha] pull v

drapplitaður [drapplita-thur] beige adj

dráttarbíll [drouttarbe-addl] tow truck

drekka [drecka] drink v

drykkur [drickur] drink n

drykkjalisti [drickjalisti] drink menu

drykkjarvatn [drickjar-vatn] drinking water

drengur [dreyngur] boy

dropi [dropi] drop n (medicine)

drullusokkur [drud-dlusockur] plunger

DVD [dje vaff dje] DVD

dýr [dear] animal

dýr [dear] expensive

dýragarður [dearagarthur] zoo

dýrmætur [dearmaytur] valuable adj

dömubindi [duhmobindi] sanitary napkin

dörslag [duhrslag] colander

E

efnaklósett [ebnak-lohsett] chemical toilet

eftir hádegi [eftir houdeghi] p.m.

eftir [eftir] after

eftirlaunaþegi [eftir-luynatheghi] retired adj (from work)

eiginkona [eyghinkona] wife

eiginmaður [eyghinma-thur] husband

einhleypur [eynhleypur] single adj (person)

eitt rúm [eytt room] single room

einrit [eynrit] single print

eitt herbergi [eytt herbergi] single bed

einhver [eynhver] some (with singular nouns)

einhverjir [eynhverjir] some (with plural nouns)

einn [eydn] alone (one, one counting)

einsdagsmiði [eynsdagh-smithi] one-day (ticket)

einstefnugata [eynstebh-nugata] one-way street

einnota [eynnota] dispos-able n

einnota rakvél [eynnota rakvyel] disposable razor

eins [eyns] same adj

einu sinni [eynu sinni] once (one time)

eitur [eytur] poison n

ekkert [eckert] nothing

ekkja [eckja] widowed

ekta silfur [ekta silfur] sterling silver

elda [elda] cook v

eldavél [eldavyel] stove n

eldhús [eldhuhs] kitchen

eldhúsfilma [eldhoos-filma] kitchen foil [BE]

eldri borgari [eldri borgari] senior citizen

eldur [eldur] fire n

eldvarnarhurð [eldvard-narhurth] fire door

elska [elska] love v

[someone]

enda [enda] end v

endir [endir] end n

ending [endeang] mileage

endurhlaða [endurhlatha] recharge v

endurtaka [endurtaka] repeat v

endurvinnsla [endur-vinnsla] recycling

enginn [eynginn] no (not any)

enskur [enskur] English adj

enska [enska] English (language)

erfitt [erfitt] difficult

etanól [etanohl] surgical spirit [BE]

evra [evra] euro

eyða [eytha] delete v (computer)

eyðimörk [eythimuhrk] desert n

eyðni [eythni] AIDS

eyðublað [eythublath] form n (document)

eyra [eyra] ear

eyrnaverkur [eyrdnav-erkur] earache

eyrnalokkur [ey-rdnalockur] earring

F

faðir [fathir] father

faðma [fathma] hug v

fallegur [faddleghur] beautiful

falleg [faddlegh] beautiful

fara [fara] go v (some-where)

fara frá [fara frou] leave v (hotel)

fara úr [fara oor] leave v (plane)

fara í gegnum [fara ea gegnum] pass through v (travel)

fara í tíma [fara ea teama] take lessons

fara um borð [fara um borth] board v

fara úr [fara uhr] get off (train [bus [subway]]

---

fara út [fara uht] exit v

farangur [faroungur] baggage [BE]

farangursafgreiðsla [faroungursafgreythsla] baggage claim

farangurskerra [faroung-urskerra] luggage cart

farangursmerki [faroungursmerki] baggage claim

farangur [faroungur] luggage

farangurskerra [faroung-urskerra] luggage cart

farangursskápur [faroungursskoupur] luggage locker

farangursmiði [faroung-ursmithi] luggage ticket

farmiði aðra leiðina [farmithi athra leything] one-way ticket (train)

farrými [farreami] class n

farsími [farseami] cell phone, mobile phone [BE] **mobile phone** [BE]

farþegi [fartheghi] passenger

fatahreinsun [fatahreynsun] dry-cleaner's

fataverslun [fataverslun] clothing store

fatlaður [fatlathur] disabled adj (person), handicapped

faxa [faxa] fax v

fax [fax] fax n

faxnúmer [faxnoomer] fax number

fá [fou] receive v

fáanlegur [fouanleghur] available

ferð [ferth] trip n

ferðalag [ferthalagh] tour n, travel n, **travel** n

ferðaskrifstofa [ferthaskrifstofa] travel agency

ferðaveiki [ferthaveyki] travel sickness

---

ferðatékki [ferthatyecki] travellers check [cheque BE]

ferðamaður [ferthama-thur] tourist

ferðamannaupplýsingar tourist information office [ferthamannuyplea-seangar]

ferðamannastaður [ferthamannastathur] attraction (place)

ferðaveiki [ferthaveyki] motion sickness

ferja [ferja] ferry n

ferskur [ferskur] fresh

ferðataska [ferthataska] suitcase

filma [filma] film n (camera)

frímerki [freamerki] stamp n (postage)

fingur [feangur] finger n

fingurnögl [feangurnuhgl] finger nail

fitulaus [fituluys] fat free

fjall [fjaddl] mountain

fjallahjól [fjaddlahjohl] mountain bike

fjarsýnn [fjarseadn] long-sighted

fjólublár [fjohlublour] purple adj

fjölskylda [fjuhlskylda] family n

flaska [flaska] bottle n

flass myndataka [flass mindataka] flash photography

fljótur [fljohtur] fast adj

flogaveikur [floghaveykur] epileptic adj

flogaveiki [floghaveyki] epileptic n

flug [flugh] flight n

flugfélag [flughfyelagh] airline

flugpóstur [flughpohstur] airmail

flugstöð [flughstuhth] terminal n (airport)

flugvél [flughvyel] airplane

flugvöllur [flughvuhddlur] airport

flugvél [flughvyel] plane n

fornmunabúð [fornmuna-booth] antiques store

forréttur [forryettur] appetizer, starter [BE]

foss [foss] waterfall

fótboltaleikur [fohtboltaleykur] football game [BE]

fótsnyrting [fohtsnirte-ang] pedicure n

fótur [fohtur] foot n, leg n **eg** n

framkalla [framkaddla] develop v (film)

framkvæmdastjóri [framkvaymdastjohri] manager

frí [frea] holiday [BE], vacacion

frjáls [frjouls] free adj

froða [frotha] mousse (hair)

frosinn matur [frosinn matur] frozen food

frystir [fristir] freezer

fugl [fugl] bird

fundur [fundur] meeting n (business)

fundarherbergi [fundar-herbergi] meeting room

furðulegur [furthulegur] amazing

fylla [filla] fill v (car)

fylla út [fiddla uht] fill out v (form)

fylling [fiddleang] filling n (tooth)

fyrir [firir] before, for

fyrir aftan [firir aftan] behind (direction)

fyrsta farrými [fyrsta farreami] first class

fyrstur [firstur] first adj

færiband [fayriband] conveyor belt

föt [fuht] clothing, suit

G

gaffall [gaffaddl] fork n

gallabuxur [gallabuxur] jeans

gamall [gamaddl] old adj

ganga [gounga] walk v

göngutúr [guhngutoor] walk n

gönguleið [guhnguleyth] walking route

gangur [goungur] aisle

gangsæti [goungsayti] aisle seat

garður [garthur] park n

gatnamót [gatnamoht] intersection

gefa [gefa] give v

geisladiskur [geisladis-kur] CD

gel [gel] gel n (hair)

gengi [gengi] exchange rate

gengilbeina [geyngil-beyna] waitress

gera við [gera vith] repair v

gervigómur [gervigohmur] denture

getnaðarlimur [getna-tharlimur] penis

giftast [giftast] marry

giftur [giftur] married

gil [gil] ravine

gildi [gildi] value n

gildur [gildur] valid

gistiheimili [gistiheymili] bed and breakfast

gjald [gjald] fee n

gjaldkeri [gjaldkeri] cashier

gjaldmiðill [gjaldmithill] currency

gjaldeyrisviðskipti [gjaldeyrisvithskifti] currency exchange

gjaldeyrisskiptastöð [gjaldeyrisskiftastuhth] currency exchange office

gjaldeyrisskipti [gjal-deyrisskifti] exchange n (place)

gjöf [gjuhf] gift n

gjafaverslun [gjafaver-slun] gift shop

glas [glas] glass (drinking)

gler [gler] glass material

gleraugu [gleruygu] glasses

gleypa [gleypa] swallow v

gljúfur [gljoofur] canyon

gluggi [gluggi] window

gluggakarmur [glugga-karmur] window case

glæsilegur [ghlaysileghur] stunning

golf [golf] golf n

golfvöllur [golfvuhddlur] golf course

golfmót [golfmoht] golf tournament

gönguleiðakort [guhngu-leythakort] trail map

gosbrunnur [gosbrunnur] fountain n

góður [gohthur] good adj, nice

gott [gott] good adj

gott kvöld [gott kvuhld] good afternoon) evening

góðan dag [gohthan dagh] good morning) day

gramm [gramm] gram

grasagarður [grasagar-thur] botanical garden

gráða [groutha] degree (temperature)

grár [grour] gray adj

greiða [greitha] comb n

grill [grill] barbecue (device) n

grænmetis [graynmetis] vegetarian n

grænmetisæta [graynmetisayta] vegetation adj

grænn [graynn] green adj

gufubað [gufubath] sauna

gull [guddl] gold n

gulur [gulur] yellow adj

gæði [gaythi] quality n

gæslumaður [gaysluma-thur] lifeguard

gönguskór [guhnguskohr] hiking boots

H

hafa [hafa] have v

hafa samband [hafa samband] contact v

hafna [habna] decline v (credit card)

halló [halloh] hello

hamar [hamar] hammer n

hamingjusamur [hameangjusamur] happy

handfarangur [handfaroungur] hand carry-on luggage

handklæði [handklaythi] towel n

handleggur [handleggur] arm n (body part)

handsnyrting [handsnyr-teang] manicure n

handtaska [handtaska] handbag

handþvottur [handthvot-tur] handwash

hattur [hattur] hat

hádegi [houdeghi] noon n

hádegismatur [houde-ghismatur] lunch n

hálfur [houlfur] half adj

hálftími [houlfteami] half hour

hálft kíló [houlft kealoh] half kilo

háls [houls] neck n, throat

hálsbindi [houlsbindi] tie n (clothing)

hálsbólga [houlsbohlga] sore throat

hálsklútur [houlskluhtur] scarf

hálsmen [houlsmen] necklace

hár [hour] hair

hárbursti [hourbursti] hairbrush

hárþurrka [hourthurrka] hairdryer

hárgreiðslustofa [hourgreythslustofa] hair salon

hársprey [hoursprey] hairspray

hártíska [hourteaska] hairstyle

hársnyrtir [hoursnirtir] hair stylist

hárnæring [hournayreang] conditioner (hair)

háskólanemi [houskohlanemi] student (university)

háskóli [houskohli]

university
hátt [houtt] high
hásæti [housayti] high chair
hefðbundinn [hefthbundinn] traditional
heilsa [heylsa] health
heilsufæðisverslun [heylsufaythisverslun] healthy food store
heilsulind [heylsulind] spa
heimamaður [heymamathur] local n (person)
heimilishald [heymilishald] housekeeping services
heimilisfang [heymilisfoung] address n
heimilisvörur [heymilisvuhrur] household goods
heimkoma [heymkoma] return n (BÉ] (trip)
heimsókn [heymsohkn] visit v
heimsóknartími [heymsohknarteami] visiting hours
heitt [heytt] warm adj (temperature)
heitur [heytur] hot (temperature)
heitur hver [heytur hver] hot spring
heitt vatn [heytt vatn] hot water
hektari [hektari] hectare
helgi [helgi] week**end**
helgidómur [helgidohmur] shrine
hellir [hellir] cave n
helmingur [helmeangur] half n
helstu leiðir [helstu leythir] main course
helstu skoðunarstaðir main attraction [helstu skothunarstathir]
hendi [hendi] hand n
herbergi [herbergi] room n
herbergislykill [herbergislykiddl] room key
herbergisþjónusta [herbergisthjonnusta]

room service
hestastigur [hestasteaghur] horsetrack
heymæði [heymaythi] hay fever
heyrnarlaus [heyrdnarluys] deaf adj
heyrnarskertur [heyrdnarskertur] hearing impaired
heyrnartól [heyrdnartohl] headphones
hér [hyer] here
hita [hita] heat v, warm v
hitari [hitari] heater
hitaeining [hitaeyneang] calorie
hiti [hiti] fever n
hitta [hitta] meet v
hjarta [hjarta] heart
hjartveiki [hjartveyki] heart condition
hjálmur [hjoulmur] helmet
hjálpa [hjoulpa] help v
hjálp [hjoulp] help n
hjólastóll [hjolastohddl] wheelchair
hjólastólarampur [hjohlastohlarampur] wheelchair ramp
hjólbarði [hjohlbarthi] tire n, tyre [BÉ]
hjólreiðar [hjohlreithar] cycling
hjúkrunarfræðingur nurse n [hjuhkrunarfraytheangur]
hlið [hlith] gate (airport), side n
hlífðardúkur [hleaftharduhkur] groundcloth
hljómsveit [hljomhsveyt] orchestra
hlutur [hlutur] part (for car)
í hlutastarfi [ea hlutastarfi] part time
hnefaleikakeppni [hnefaleykakeppni] boxing match
hné [hnye] knee n
hnífur [hneafur] knife
hokkí [hockea] hockey

hommabar [hommabar] gay bar
hommaklúbbur [hommakloobbur] gay club
horfa [horfa] watch v
hornabolti [hordnabolti] baseball
hópur [hohpur] group n
hósta [hohsta] cough v
hósti [hohsti] cough n
hótel [hohtel] hotel
hraðvagn [hrathvagn] express bus
hraðlest [hrathlest] express train
hraðakstur [hrathakstur] speeding
hraðbanki [hrathbanki] ATM
hraðbankakort [hrathbankakort] ATM card
hraðbraut [hrathbruyt] motorway [BE]
hreinsa [hreynsa] clean v
hrein [hreyn] clean adj (clothes)
hreinsivara [hreynsivara] cleaning product
hreinsa [hreynsa] clear v (on an ATM)
hressilegur [hressileghur] spicy (not bland)
hreyfanleiki [hreyfanleyki] mobility
hringferð [hreangferth] round trip
hringja [hreangja] call v (phone)
hringja á kostnað viðtakanda call collect [hreangja ou kostnath vithtakanda]
hringja [hreangja] dial v, phone v
hringur [hreangur] ring n
hryggur [hriggur] spine (body part)
hræðilegur [hraythileghur] terrible
hurð [hurth] door
húð [huhth] skin n
hús [huhs] house n
húsbíll [huhsbeaddl]

mobile home
húsnæði [hoosnaythi] accommodation
hvað [hvath] what
hvar [hvar] where
hvenær [hvenayr] when adv (at that time)
hver [hver] who (question)
hvernig [hverdnigh] how
hve mikið [hve mikith] how much
hvítur [hveatur] white adj
hvítagull [hveatuguddl] white gold
hæ [hay] hi
hæð [hayth] floor n (level), storey [BE] híí in house
hægari [hayghari] slower
hægðir [hayghthir] stool (bowel movement)
hægri [hayghri] right adj, adv (direction)
hægri réttur [hayghri ryettur] right of way
hægt [haygt] slowly
hærra [hayrra] louder
hætta við [haytta vith] cancel
hættulegur [hayttuleghur] dangerous
höfuð [huhfuth] head (body part) n
höfuðverkur [huhfuthverkur] headache
höll [huhddl] palace

ilmolíumeðferð [ilmoleaumethferth] aromatherapy
ilmvatn [ilmvatn] cologne, perfume n
innbrot [innbrot] break-in n
innanlands [innanlands] domestic
innanlandsflug [innanlandsflugh] domestic flight
inngangur [inngoungur] entrance
innifela [innifela] include v
inniskór [inniskohr]

loafers, slippers
innistæða [innistaytha]
deposit n (bank)
innisundlaug [in-
nisundluygh] indoor pool
(public)
innkaup [innkuyp]
shopping n
innrita [innrita] check v
(luggage)
innritun [innritun]
check-in
innskráning [innskroune-
ang] log on v (computer)
insúlín [insuhlean] insulin
internet [internet] internet
í [ea] in
í dag [ea dagh] today adv
í gær [ea gayr] yesterday
adv
í kvöld [ea kvuhld] tonight
í lagi [ea laghi] OK
í raspi [ea raspi] breaded
íbúð [eabouth] apartment
**íbúi á Evrópusambandss-
vædinu** EU resident
[eabuhi ou Evrohpusam-
bandssvaythinu]
íbúprófen [eabuhprohfen]
ibuprofen
Írland [earland] Ireland
írskur [earskur] Irish adj
ís [eas] ice n
íshokkí [eashockea] ice
hockey
ískaldur [easkaldur] icy
ísskápur [easskoupur]
refrigerator
ítalskur [eatalskur]
Italian adj
íþróttaskór [eathroht-
taskohr] sneakers
íþróttir [eathrohttir] sports
íþróttanudd [eathrohtta-
nudd] sports massage

J

jafningi [jabneangi]
match n
jakki [jacki] jacket n
japanskur [japanskur]
Japanese adj
jarðhæð [jarthhayth]

ground floor
já [jou] yes
járn [jourdn] iron v

K

kabarett [kabarett]
cabaret
kafa [kafa] dive v
kafarabúnaður
[kafarabuhnathur] diving
equipment
kaffihús [kaffihoos] cafe
(place)
kaldur [kaldur] cold adj
(temperature)
Kanada [Kanada] Canada
kanadískur [kanadeaskur]
Canadian adj
kappakstursbraut
[kappakstursbruyt]
racetrack
karafla [karafla] carafe
karfa [karfa] basket
(grocery store)
karton [karton] carton (of
cigarettes)
kasta upp [kasta upp]
vomit v
kastar upp [kastar upp]
vomiting
kastali [kastali] castle
kaupa [kuypa] buy v
kennslustund [kennslus-
tund] lesson n
kerra [kerra] cart (grocery
store), trolley [BE]
kíló [kealoh] kilo
kílógramm [kealohgramm]
kilogram
kílómeter [kealohmeter]
kilometer
kínverskur [keanverskur]
Chinese adj
kjálki [kjoulki] jaw n
kjóll [kjohddl] dress
(clothing)
klassísk tónlist [klas-
seask tohnlist] classical
music
klaustur [kluystur]
monastery
kláfferja [kloufferja]
cable car

klipping [klippeang] haircut
klukkustund [kluckus-
tund] hour
klúbbur [kloobbur] club n
klæðaburður [klaythabur-
thur] dress code
knattspyrna [knatt-
spyrdna] soccer
koddi [koddi] pillow n
koma [koma] arrival,
arrive, come
koma inn [koma inn] enter
v (place)
koma með [koma meth]
bring
kona [kona] woman
kopar [kopar] copper n
korktappi [korktappi]
corkscrew n
kort [kort] card n
koss [koss] kiss v
kosta [kosta] cost v
kreditkort [kreditkort]
credit card
krem [krem] cream
(ointment)
kringum [kreangum]
around the corner
kristall [kristall] crystal
n (glass)
krukka [krucka] jar (for
jam etc.)
kryddaður [kriddathur]
spicy
kústur [koostur] broom
kvarta [kvarta] complaint
kvef [kvef] cold n
(sickness)
kveikja á [kveykja ou] turn
on v (device)
kveikja í [kveykja ea]
light n (cigarette)
kvensjúkdómafræðingur
gynecologist
[kvensjuhk-
dohmafraytheangur]
kvittun [kvittun] receipt n
kvöld [kvuhld] evening n
kvöldmatur [kvuhldmatur]
dinner
kynna [kinna] introduce v
(person)
kynsjúkdómur [kyn-

sjuhkdohmur] sexually
transmitted
disease (STD)
kærasta [kayrasta]
girlfriend
kærasti [kayrasti]
boyfriend
körfubolti [kuhrvubolti]
basketball

L

laga [lagha] fix v (repair)
lak [lak] sheet n (bed)
laktósaóþol [laktohs-
aohthol] lactose
intolerant
landakort [landakort]
map n
landsnúmer [lands-
noomer] country code
langt í burtu [loungt ea
burtu] far (distance)
langur [loungur] long adj
langerma [langerma]
long-sleeved
laug [luygh] pool n
laus [luys] loose (fit)
lausavinna [luysavinna]
freelance work
laust [luyst] vacancy
(room)
lágur [loughur] low adj
léður [lethur] leather n
leggja [leggja] park v
leggja inn [leggja inn]
deposit v (money)
leið [leyth] line n (train
[bus], route n
leiðarvísir [leytharveasir]
guide n (book)
leiðsögumaður [leyth-
suhghumathur] guide n
(person)
leiðsöguhundur
[leythsuhghuhundur]
guide dog
leiðinlegur [leythinleghur]
boring
leigja [leyghja] rent v
leiga [leygha] rent n
leigubíll [leyghubeaddl]
taxi n
leikfang [leykfoung] toy

leikfangaverslun
[leykfoungaverslun]
toy store

leikgrind [leykgrind]
playpen

leikhús [leykhuhs] theater

leikrit [leykrit] play n
(theatre)

leikur [leykur] game n

leikvöllur [leykvuhddlur]
playground

leirkeragerð [leyrker-
agerth] pottery

leita að einhverju [leyta
ath einhverju] look for
something

lest [lest] train n

lestarstöð [lestarstuhth]
train station

lestarstöð [lestarstuhth]
railway station [BE]

leyfa [leyfa] allow, permit v

leyfilegt [leyfilegt] halal,
kosher adj

létt bifhjól [lyett bifhjohl]
moped

léttari [lyettari] lighter n

lið [lith] team n

liðagigt [lithagigt]
arthritis

liður [lithur] joint n (body
part)

lifa [lifa] live v

lifandi tónlist [lifandi
tohnlist] live music

lifur [lifur] liver (body part)

linsa [linsa] lens

list [list] art

litur [litur] color n

lika við [leaka vith] like v

lita [leata] look v

litill [leatiddl] little, small

litri [leatri] liter

ljós [ljohs] light n (overhead)

ljósapera [ljohsapera]
lightbulb

ljósmynd [ljohsmind]
photo

ljósrit [ljohsrit] photocopy

ljósmyndun [ljohs-
myndun] photography

ljótur [ljohtur] ugly

ljúffengt [ljuhffeyngt]
delicious

loft [loft] air n

loftræsting [loftraysteang]
air conditioning

loftþurrka [loftthurrka]
air dry

loftdæla [loftdayla]
air pump

loka [loka] close v (a shop)

lokuð [lokuth] closed

lungu [loongu] lung

lúxusbifreið [luhxusbi-
freyth] luxury car

lyf [lif] medicine

lyfjameðferð [lyfjameth-
ferth] medication (drugs)

lyfseðill [lifsethiddl]
prescription

lyfta [lifta] elevator,
lift [BE]

lyftuferð [lyftuferth] lift
n (ride)

lyftumiði [lyftumithi]
lift pass

lykill [likiddl] key n

lyklakippa [lyklakippa]
keyring

lykilorð [likilorth] password

lýsing [leaseang] exposure
(film)

læknir [layknir] doctor n

lækur [laykur] stream n

læri [layri] thigh

lærir [layrir] studying n

læsa [laysa] lock v

lás [lous] lock n

lögfræðingur [luhgfray-
theanghur] lawyer n

lögregla [luhghregla]
police

lögregluskýrsla
[luhghreghluskearsla]
police report

lögreglustöð [luhghre-
glustuhth] police station

M

maður [mathur] man
(adult male)

magi [maghi] stomach

magaverkur [ma-
ghaverkur] stomachache

markaður [markathur]
market n

mata [mata] feed v

matprjónar [matprjohnar]
chopsticks

matprjónn [matprjohnn]
church

matseðill [matsethiddl]
menu (restaurant)

**matseðill með föstu
verði** [matsethiddl meth fuhstu
verthi] fixed price menu

matur [matur] food

matvinnsluvél
[matvinnsluvyel] food
processor

matvöruverslun
[matvuhruverslun]
grocery store

má setja í þvottavél
[mou setja ea thvottavyel]
machine washable

máltíð [moulteath] meal

mánuður [mounuthur]
month

mátunarklefi [moutunar-
klefi] fitting room

með [meth] with

með asma [meth asma]
asthmatic

með hægðatregðu
[meth haygthatregthu]
constipated

meðlæti [methlayti]
side dish

meðlætispöntun [methlay-
tispuhntun] side order

með ofnæmi [meth
ofnaymi] allergic

meðmæli [methmayli]
recommendation

meðvitundarlaus
[methvitundarluys]
unconscious (faint)

meiða [meytha] hurt v

meira [meyra] more

messa [messa] mass n
(church service)

miðbær [mithbayr]
downtown n

miðdegi [mithdeghi]
midday [BE]

miði [mithi] ticket

miðasala [mithasala]
ticket office

miðlungs [mithloongs]
medium (steak)

miðnætti [mithnaytti]
midnight

millifæra [middlifayra]
transfer money

millilandaflug [middlilan-
daflugh] international
flight

millistig [middlistigh]
intermediate

millistykki [millistikki]
adapter

minibar [meaneabar]
minibar

minjagripur [minja-
gripur] souvenir n

minjagripaverslun
[minjagripaverslun]
souvenir store

minna [minna] less

minniskort [minniskort]
memory card

minnisvarði [minnisvarthi]
memorial (place)

mistök [mistuhk] mistake n

mínúta [meanuhta] minute

moppa [moppa] mop n

morgunn [morgunn]
morning n

morgunverður [morgun-
verthur] breakfast n

moska [moska] mosque

móðir [mohthir] mother n

Mótmælandi [Mohtmay-
landi] Protestant

mótor [mohtor] motor n

mótorbátur [mohtorbou-
tur] motorboat

mótorhjól [mohtorhjohl]
motorcycle

móttaka [mohttaka]
reception (hotel)

munnur [munnur] mouth n

musteri [musteri] temple
(religious)

myndavél [mindavyel]
camera

myndavélataska
[myndavyelataska]
camera case

mynt [mint] coin
mæla [mayla] measure v (someone)
mæla með [mayla meth] recommend
mæliglas [mayliglas] measuring cup
mælir [maylir] meter in (parking)
metri [metri] meter n (measure)
mæliskeið [mayliskeyth] measuring spoon

N

nafn [nabn] name n
naglasnyrtistofa [naglas-nyrtistofa] nail salon
naglaþjöl [naglathjuhl] nail file
nafnspjald [nabnspjald] business card
nauðga [nuythga] rape v
nauðgun [nuythgun] rape n
ná [nou] reach v
nálastungulækningar acupuncture [noulastoongulaykneangar]
nálægt [noulaygt] near
nálægt [noulaygt] nearby
námskeið [noumskeyth] seminar
náttföt [nouttfuht] pajamas
náttúruverndarsvæði nature preserve [nouttuhruverndarsvaythi]
nemandi [nemandi] university
neðanjarðar [nethanjar-thar] underground n [BE]
neðanjarðarstöð [nethanjartharstuhth] underground station [BE]
nef [nef] nose
nei [ney] no
nestisferðasvæði [nestisferthasvaythi] picnic area
netfang [netfoung] e-mail address
netkaffihús [netkaffihoos] internet cafe

netþjónusta [netthjoh-nusta] internet service
neyðartilvik [neythartil-vik] emergency
neyðarútgangur [neytharootgoungur] emergency exit
niðurgangur [nithurgoun-gur] diarrhea
niðursuðuvörur [nithurs-uthuvuhrur] canned good
njóta [njohta] enjoy
norður [northur] north n
nota [nota] use v
notandanafn [notandan-abn] username
nótt [nohtt] night
næturklúbbur [nayturk-loobbur] nightclub
nudd [nudd] massage n
númer [nuhmer] number in
driver's license number [nuhmer uhkuskearteynis]
nýliði [nealithi] novice
nýra [neara] kidney (body part)
næla [nayla] brooch
nærbuxur [nayrbuxur] underpants [BE]
nærföt [nayrfuht] underwear
næstur [naystur] next adj
nærsýnn [nayrseadn] near-sighted

O

of litið eldaður [of leatith eldathur] underdone
ofan við [ofan vith] over prep (direction)
ofeldaður [ofeldathur] ~done (meat)
ofhitaður [ofhitathur] ~heat v (car)
ofnæmisviðbrögð [ofnaymisvithbruhgdth] allergic reaction
olía [oleaa] oil n
olnbogi [olnbogi] elbow n
opinber [opinber] public adj

opna [opna] open v
opinn [opinn] open adj
ódýr [ohdear] inexpensive
ódýrt [ohdeart] cheap
ódýrara [ohdearara] cheaper
óglatt [ohglatt] nauseous
ógleði [ohglethi] nausea
ópera [ohpera] opera
óperuhús [ohperuhoos] opera house
opnunartimi [opnunar-teami] business **hours**
órólegur í maganum upset stomach [ohrohleghur ea maghanum]
óskilamunir [ohskilamu-nir] lost and found
óvörumerkt lyf [ohvuhrumerkt lyf] unbranded medication [BE]

P

padda [padda] bug (insect) n
pakka [packa] pack v
pakka inn [packa inn] wrap v
pakki [packi] package n
pantanaborð [pantan-aborth] reservation desk
pallur [paddlur] platform [BE] (train)
panta [panta] reserve v (hotel)
pappakassi [pappakassi] carton (of groceries)
pappír [pappear] paper n (material)
pappírsþurrka [pap-pearsthurrka] tissue, paper towel
parasetamól [paraseta-mohl] paracetamol [BE]
passa [passa] fit n (clothing)
peli [peli] baby bottle
peningar [peneangar] cash n, money
penni [penni] pen n
pensillín [pensillean]

penicillin
perla [perla] pearl n
peysa [peysa] sweater, sweatshirt
pilla [pilla] Pill (birth control)
pils [pils] skirt n
pitsustaður [peatsusta-thur] pizzeria
pjatla [pjatla] patch v (clothing)
plastumbúðir [plastum-buhthir] plastic wrap
platína [plateana] platinum n
poki [poki] bag
popptónlist [popptohnlist] pop music
pottur [pottur] pot n
póstur [pohstur] post n [BE]
pósthús [pohsthoos] post office
pósthólf [pohsthohlf] postbox [BE]
póstkort [pohstkort] postcard
prenta [prenta] print v
prent [prent] print n
pressa [pressa] press v (clothing)
pund [pund] pound n (weight or British sterling)
púði [puhthi] pad n [BE]
pöntun [puhntun] order v (restaurant) reservation

R

rafhlaða [rafhlatha] battery
rafmagnsinnstunga [rafmagnsinnstoonga] electric outlet
rakari [rakari] barber
raksápa [raksoupa] shav-ing cream
rakspíri [rakspeari] aftershave
rakvélablað [rakvyelab-lath] razor blade
rannsókn [rannsohkn] study v n
rapp [rapp] rap n (music)
rass [rass] buttocks

rauður [ruythur] red adj
raunverulegur [ruynver-uleghur] real adj
ráðast á [routhast ou] attack v
ráðgjafi [routhgjafi] consultant
ráðhús [routhhoos] town hall
ráðstefna [routhstebna] conference
ráðstefnusalur [routhstebnusalur] convention hall
regnhlíf [regnhleaf] umbrella
regnkápa [regnkoupa] raincoat
regnskógur [regnskoghur] rainforest
reiðhjól [reithhjol] bicycle
reiðhjólastígur [reithhjolasteaghur] bike route
reikningur [reykneangur] account n (bank) invoice n [BE] bill (of sale)
reykingasvæði [reykeangasvaythi] smoking (area)
reykja [reykja] smoke v
reyklaus [reykluys] non smoking adj
reyndur [reyndur] experienced
rifbein [rifbeyn] rib n (body part)
rigning [rigneang] rain n
rólegur [rohleghur] quiet adj
rómantískur [rohmanteaskur] romantic adj
ruðningur [ruthneangur] rugby
rusl [rusl] rubbish n [BE]
ruslapoki [ruslapoki] rubbish) garbage bag
rusl [rusl] trash n
rúllustigi [ruhllustighi] escalator
rúm [room] bed n
rúmföt [ruhmfuht] linen
rúst [ruhst] ruin n
ryksuga [riksugha] vacuum cleaner
ræðismannsskrifstofa

ræðismannsskrifstofa consulate [raythismannsskrifstofa]
rækt [raykt] gym n (place)
ræna [rayna] mug v, rob v
rændur [rayndur] robbed

S

safn [sabn] museum
salerni [salerdni] restroom
salerni [salerdni] toilet [BE]
salernispappír [salerdnis-pappear] toilet paper
samband [samband] relationship
samheitalyf [samheitalif] generic drug
samkynhneigður [samkinhneighthur] gay adj (homosexual)
samstarfsmaður [samstarfsmathur] colleague
samtals [samtals] total n (amount)
samþykkja [samthickja] accept v, confirm
sandalar [sandalar] sandals
sandali [sandali] flip flops
sápa [soupa] soap n
sáraumbúðir [souraum-boothir] bandage
sársauki [soursuyki] pain
seðill [sethiddl] bill n (money), note (money) [BE]
seigur [seyghur] tough adj (food)
seinn [seynn] late (time)
sekt [sekt] fine n (fee for breaking law)
selja [selja] sell v
senda [senda] send v
senda með hraði [senda meth hrathi] express adj
senda póst [senda pohst] mail v
senda tölvupóst [senda tuhlvupohst] e-mail v
sendibíll [sendibeaddl] van
sentimetri [senteametri] centimeter

sjálfsþjónusta [sjoulfsth-johnusta] self service
servíetta [serveaetta] napkin
sérfræðingur [syerfray-theangur] expert
sérfræðingur [syerfray-theangur] specialist (doctor)
stuttermabolur [stut-termabolur] T-shirt
síðdegi [seathdeghi] afternoon
silfur [silfur] silver n
silki [silki] silk
sitja [sitja] sit v
síðastur [seathastur] last adj
símakort [seamakort] phone card
símanúmer [seamanoo-mer] phone number
sími [seami] telephone n, phone
símtal [seamtal] call n
sjaldgæfur [sjaldgayfur] rare
sjampó [sjampoh] shampoo n
sjá [sjou] see v
sjálfvirkur [sjoulfvirkur] automatic
sjálfskiptur bíll [sjoulfskiftur beaddl] automatic car
sjóða [sjohtha] boil v
sjónskertur [sjohnsker-tur] visually impaired
sjónvarp [sjohnvarp] TV
sjór [sjohr] sea
sjúkrabíll [sjookrabe-addl] ambulance
sjúkrahús [sjuhkrahuhs] hospital
skammtur [skammtur] portion n
skanni [skanni] scanner
skartgripasali [skartgri-pasali] jeweler
skartgripir [skartgripir]

jewelry
skál [skoul] bowl n
skál! [skoul!] Cheers!
skápur [skoupur] locker
skeið [skeyth] spoon n
skemma [skemma] damage v
skemmtigarðaur [skemmtigarthur] amusement park
skemmtun [skemmtun] entertainment
skera [skera] cut v
skurður [skurthur] cut n (injury)
skila [skila] return v (something)
skilaboð [skilaboth] message
skilinn [skilinn] separated (person)
skilja [skilja] divorce v
skilja [skilja] understand v
skip [skip] ship v
skipta [skifta] exchange v, cash v
skipta á [skifta ou] change v (baby)
skipta um [skifta um] transfer v (change trains (flights)
skíða [skeatha] ski v
skíði [skeathi] ski n
skíðalyfta [skeathalyfta] ski lift
skítugur [skeatughur] dirty
skjár [skjour] display n (device)
skoðunarferð [skothu-narferth] excursion
skoðunarferðir [skothunarferthir] sightseeing
skoðunarferð [skothunarferth] sightseeing tour
skordýr [skordear] insect
skordýrabit [skordeara-bit] insect bite
skordýraeitur [skordear-aeytur] insect repellent
skóbúð [skohbuhth]

shoe store
skógur [skohghur] forest n
skóli [skohli] school n
skór [skohr] shoe
skráning ökutækis [skrouneang uhkutaykis] vehicle registration
skrifa [skrifa] write v
skrifstofa [skrifstofa] office
skrifstofutími [skrifstofuteami] office hours
skuldfæra [skuldfayra] charge v (credit card)
skyrta [skirta] shirt
skæri [skayri] scissors
slagæð [slagayð] artery
slátrari [sloutrari] butcher n
slóð [slohth] path
slóð [slohth] trail n (ski)
slys [slis] accident
slökkva á [sluhckva ou] turn off v (device)
slökkvilið [sluhckvilith] fire department
smitaður [smitathur] infected
smitandi [smitandi] contagious
smokkur [smockur] condom
snarl [snarl] snack bar
sneið [sneyth] slice n
snemma [snemma] early
snjóbretti [snjohbretti] snowboard n
snjóbrúga [snjohthruhgha] snowshoe n
snudda [snudda] soother [BE]
snuð [snuth] pacifier
snyrta [snirta] trim (hair) v
snævi þakinn [snayvi thakinn] snowy
snöggsteikja [snuhggsteykja] sauté v
sofa [sofa] sleep v
sokkabuxur [sockabuxur] pantyhose
sokkabuxur [sockabuxur] tights [BE]

sokkur [sockur] sock
sól [sohl] sun n
sólarvörn [sohlarvuhrn] sunblock
sólbruni [sohlbruni] sunburn
sólgleraugu [sohlghleruyghu] sunglasses
sólríkt [sohlreakt] sunny
sólhlíf [sohlhlaf] sunscreen
sólstingur [sohlsteangur] sunstroke
sótthreinsandi krem [sohtthreynsandi krem] antiseptic cream
sótthreinsandi vökvi [sohtthreynsandi vuhkvi] rubbing alcohol
spaði [spathi] spatula
sparnaður [spardnathur] savings (account)
spor [spor] track n (train)
spurning [spurdneang] question n
stafa [stafa] spell v
stafrænt [stafraynt] digital
stafræn myndavél [stafrayn myndavyel] digital camera
stafræn ljósmynd [stafrayn ljohsmynd] digital photo
stafræn prentun [stafrayn prentun] digital print
stefnumót [stebnumoht] appointment
steikarpanna [steykarpanna] frying pan
steikhús [steykhuhs] steakhouse
stela [stela] steal v
sterkur [sterkur] hot (spicy)

stigi [stighi] stairs
stimpill [stimpiddl] stamp v (ticket)
stingur [steangur] sting n
stífla [steafla] congestion (medical)
stígvél [steagvyel] boot n
stolinn [stolinn] stolen
stóll [stohddl] chair n
stólalyfta [stohlalifta] chairlift
stór [stohr] big
stærri [stayrri] bigger
stór [stohr] large
stórkostlegt [stohrkostleght] magnificent
stríðsminnisvarði [streathsminnisvarthi] war memorial
stroffhálsmál [stroffhoulsmoul] crew neck
straujárn [struyjourdn] iron clothes
strætó [straytoh] bus n
strætóstöð [straytohstohth] bus station
stoppistöð [stoppistuhth] bus stop
strætómiði [straytohmithi] bus ticket
strætóleið [straytohleyth] bus tour
strönd [struhnd] beach
stunda kynlíf [stunda kynleaf] have sex
sturta [sturta] shower n (bath)
stutt [stutt] short
stutterma [stutterma] short-sleeved
stuttar nærbuxur [stuttar nayrbuxur] briefs (clothing)
stuttbuxur [stuttbuxur] shorts
stúlka [stuhlka] girl
stykki [sticki] piece n
stytta [stitta] statue
stærð [stayrth] size n
stöð [stuhth] station n (stop)

stöðumælir [stuhthumaylir] parking meter
stöðuvatn [stuhthuvatn] lake
stöðva [stuhthva] stop v (bus)
stoppistöð [stoppistuhth] stop n (transportation)
stöng [stuhng] poles (skiing)
sundföt [sundfuht] swimsuit
suður [suthur] south n
suðutæki [suthutayki] camping stove
súper [suhper] super n (fuel)
stórmarkaður [stohrmarkathur] supermarket
súrefnismeðferð [suhrebnismethferth] oxygen treatment
svalur [svalur] cool adj (temperature)
svangur [svoungur] hungry
svartur [svartur] black adj
svefnleysi [svebnleysi] insomnia
svefnsalur [svebnsalur] dormitory
svefnvagn [svebnvagn] sleeping car [BE] sleeper car
svefnpoki [svebnpoki] sleeping bag
svima [svima] dizzy adj
svitalyktareyðir [svitaliktareithir] deodorant
svæði [svaythi] region
svæðisnúmer [svæthisnoomer] area code
syfja [sifja] drowsiness
sykursjúkur [sikursjuhkur] diabetic adj n
sykursýki [sykurseaki]
synda [sinda] swim v
systir [sistir] sister
syking í leggöngum [seakeangh ea leghghuhnghum] vaginal infection

sýklalyf [seaklalif]
antibiotic n

sýna [seana] show v

syningarkassi [seanean-garkassi] display case

sýnishorn [seanishordn]
specimen

sækja [saykja] pick up v
(person)

sælgæti [saylgayti] candy

sælgæti [saylgayti]
sweet n [BE]

sætur [saytur] sweet adj
(taste)

sælkerafæði [saylkera-faythi] delicatessen

sæti [teami] seat n

sætur [saytur] cute

sæþota [saythota] jet ski n

söluskattur [suhluskat-tur] sales tax

T

tafla [tafla] tablet
(medicine)

taka [taka] take v

taka bíl á leigu [taka
beal ou leyghu] hire v
[BE] (a car)

taka út [taka uht]
withdraw v (money)

tala [tala] speak v

tannkrem [tannkrem]
toothpaste

tannlæknir [tannlayknir]
dentist

tá [tou] toe n

tákn [toukn] symbol
(keyboard)

tánögl [tounuhgl] toenail

tékkareikningur
[tyeckareykneangur]
checking account

tenging [teyngeang]
connection
(travel (internet)

tengiflug [teynghiflugh]
connection flight

tengivagn [teyngivagn]
trailer (car)

tengja [teyngja] connect
(internet)

tennis [tennis] tennis

tennisspaði [tennis-spathi] racket n (sports)

teppi [teppi] blanket

teskeið [teskeyth]
teaspoon

texta [texta] text v (send
a message)

texti [texti] text n

texti [texti] subtitle n

textastöð [textastuhth]
subtitle station

rafrænn farseðill
[rafraynn farsethiddl]
e-ticket

til [til] to (direction)

tilbúinn [tilbuhinn] ready

tilkynna [tilkinna]
declare v (customs)

tilkynna [tilkinna]
notify v

timburmenn [timbur-menn] hangover

sivirkur [seavirkur] full
time adj

tindur [tindur] peak n (of
a mountain)

tíðakrampi [teathakram-pi] menstrual cramps

tíðatappi [teathatappi]
tampon n

tíðir [teathir] period
(menstrual)

tímabil [timabil]
period (of time)

tímabundið [teamabun-dith] temporary

tímarit [teamarit]
magazine

tímatafla [teamatafla]
timetable [BE]
(transportation)

tími [teami] time

tjald [tjald] tent n

tjaldhæll [tjaldhayddl]
tentpeg

tjaldsúla [tjaldsoola]
tentpole

tjalda [tjalda] camp v

tjaldsvæði [tjaldsvaythi]
campside

tjörn [tjuhrdn] pond n

toglyfta [toghlifta]
drag lift

togna [toggna] sprain n

tollfrjáls [toddlfrjouls]
duty-free

tollskonun [toddlskot-hun] customs

tollur [toddlur] duty (tax)

tóbakssali [tohbakssali]
tobacconist

tónleikar [tohnleikar]
concert

tónlistarhús [tohnlistar-hoos] concert hall

tónlist [tohnlist] music

tónlistarverslun
[tohnlistarverslun]
music store

tré [trye] tree

trip ticket multiple
fjölnota miði [fjuhlnota
mithi]

trúlofaður [truhlofathur]
engaged (person)

trygging [triggeang]
insurance

tryggingarskírteini
[tryggeangarskeart-eyni] insurance card

tryggingafélag
[tryggeangafyelagh]
insurance company

tunga [toonga] tongue n

turn [turdn] tower n

túlkur [tuhlkur]
interpreter

tvíbreitt rúm [tveabreytt
ruhm] double bed

tyggigúmmí [tyggigoom-mea] chewing gum

tylft [tilft] dozen

týna [teana] lose v
(something)

tynt [teant] lost

tæki [tayki] equipment

tæma [tayma] empty v

töf [tuhf] delay v

tölva [tuhlva] computer

tölvupóstur [tuhl-vupohstur] e-mail n

tönn [tuhnn] tooth

U

ull [uddl] wool

umboðsskrifstofa

[umbothsskrifstofa]
agency

umbúðafilma [umbootha-filma] cling film [BE]

umferðarljós [umfer-tharljohs] traffic light

umframfarangurs
[umframfaroungurs]
excess baggage

umframstærð [umfram-stayrth] extra large

umslag [umslagh]
envelope

um það bil [um thath bil]
around (price)

undarlegt [undarlegt]
strange

undirrita [undirrita] sign
v (document)

ungur [oongur] young adj

uppgefinn [uppgefinn]
exhausted

upphitun [upphitun]
heating [BE]

upplýsingar [upplea-seangar] information
(phone)

upplýsingaborð [up-pleaseangaborth]
information desk

uppnefndur [uppnebn-dur] dubbed

uppstoppaður [uppstop-pathur] stuffed

upptakari [upptakari]
bottle opener

uppþvottavél [uppthvot-tavyel] dishwasher

uppþvottavélasápa
[uppthvottavy-elasoupa] dishwashing
liquid

utan við [utan vith]
outside prep

úlnliður [uhlnlithur] wrist

útbrot [uhtbrot] rash n

útgangur [ootgoungur]
exit n

útisundlaug [uhtisund-luyg] outdoor pool

útskráning [uhtsk-rouneang] log off v
(computer), check-out

útsýnisstaður
[uhtseanisstathur]
viewpoint [BE]
úttekt [oottekt]
withdrawal (bank)

V

vaðtjörn [vathtjuhrdn]
paddling pool [BE]
vandamál [vandamoul]
problem
vantar [vantar] missing
(not there)
vara [vara] good n
vasaljós [vasaljohs]
flashlight
vasi [vasi] pocket n
vaskur [vaskur] sink n
vax [vax] wax v (hair)
veður [vethur] weather n
vegabréf [veghabryef]
passport
vegabréfsskoðun
[veghabryefsskothun]
passport control
vegabréfsáritun
[veghabryefsouri-
tun] visa
vegakort [vegakort]
road map
vegan [vegan] vegan n
vegan [vegan] vegan adj
vegfarandi [veghfarandi]
pedestrian n
veikur [veykur] ill
veikur [veykur] sick adj
veitingastaður [veytean-
gastathur] restaurant
vekja [vekja] wake v
vakning [vakneang]
wake-up call
velkominn [velkominn]
welcome adj
gjörðu svo vel [gjuhrthu
svo vel] you're welcome
venjulegur [venjuleghur]
regular n (fuel)
vera [vera] be v
vera samferða [vera
samfertha] join v (go
with somebody)
verkstæði [verkstaythi]
garage (for repairs)

verð [verth] price n
versla [versla] shop v
verslun [verslun] shop n
verslanaskrá [versla-
naskrou] store directory
(mall)
verslunarmiðstöð
[verslunarmithstuhth]
shopping centre [BE],
mall
verslunarsvæði
[verslunarsvaythi]
shopping area
veski [veski] wallet
vestur [vestur] west n
vélvirki [vyelvirki]
mechanic n
v-hálsmál [v-houlsmoul]
V-neck
viðskipti [vithskifti]
business adj
viðskiptamiðstöð [vith-
skiftamithstuhth]
business center
viðskiptafarrými
[vithskiftafarreami]
business class
vifta [vifta] fan n (ap-
pliance)
vika [vika] week
vikulega [vikulegha]
weekly
vínbúð [veanbuhth]
off-licence [BE]
vindill [vindiddl] cigar
vinna [vinna] work v
vinsamlegast [vinsam-
leghast] please adv
vinstri [vinstri] left adj,
adv (direction)
vinur [vinur] friend
virðisaukaskattur
[virthisuykaskattur]
VAT [BE]
virki [virki] fort
vista [vista] save v
vígvöllur [veagvuhddlur]
battleground
vínbúð [veanbuhth]
liquor store
vínekra [veanekra]
vineyard
vínlisti [veanlisti]

wine list
vísindi [veasindi] science
vítamín [veatamean]
vitamin
viðskiptafarrými
[vithskiftafarreami]
business class
vottorð [vottorth]
certificate
votviðrasamur [vot-
vithrasamur] rainy
vöðvi [vuhthvi] muscle n
völlur [vuhddlur] field
(sports)
völlur [vuhddlur] stadium
vör [vuhr] lip n

Y

yfir borðið [ifir borthith]
over the counter
(medication)
yfirhöfn [ifirhuhbn] coat
yfirsýn [yfirsean] over-
look a (a scenic place)
yfir nótt [yfir nohtt]
overnight
ýta [eata] push v

Þ

þakka [thacka] thank v
þakka þér fyrir [thacka
thyer fyrir] thank you
þar [thar] there
þarmur [tharmur]
intestine
þetta [thetta] this
þilfarsstóll [thilfarss-
tohddl] deck chair
þinghús [theanghuhs]
parliament building
þjóðerni [thjohtherdni]
nationality
þjóðlagatónlist
[thjohthlaghatohnlist]
folk music
þjófnaður [thjohbnathur]
theft
þjófur [thjohfur] thief
þjónn [thjohdn] waiter
þjónusta [thjohnusta]
service (in a restaurant)
þjóta [thjohta] rush n
þjóðvegur [thjohthve-

ghur] highway
þorp [thorp] village
þráðlaus [throuthluys]
wireless
þráðlaus sími
[throuthluys seami]
wireless phone
þreyttur [threyttur] tired
þrumuveður [thrumuve-
thur] thunderstorm
þröngur [thruhngur] tight
þurfa [thurfa] need v
þurrhreinsa [thur-
rhreynsa] dry clean
þurrka [thurrka] baby
wipe

þurrka [thurrka]
tumble dry
þvag [thvagh] urine
þvottaefni [thvottaebni]
detergent
þvottahús [thvottahuhs]
launderette [BE]
þvottahús [thvottahuhs]
laundry (place)
þvottaþjónusta [thvot-
tathjohnusta] laundry
service
þvottavél [thvottavyel]
laundromat
þvottavél [thvottavyel]
washing machine
þyrstur [thyrstur] thirsty
þýða [theatha] translate
Þýskaland [theaska-
land] Germany
þýskur [theaskur]
German adj
þýska [theaska] Ger-
man n (language)

Ö

ökkli [uhkkli] ankle
önnur leið [uhnnur leith]
alternate route
örbylgjuofn [uhrbyl-
gjuobn] microwave n
öruggur [uhruggur] safe
adj (protected)
öruggt [uhruggt] safen
(thing)
öryggi [uhryggi] security
öxl [uhxl] shoulder n

INDEX

Berlitz pocket guide

REYKJAVÍK

Second Edition 2019

Editor: Helen Fanthorpe
Author: Fran Parnell
Head of DTP and Pre-Press: Rebeka Davies
Picture Editor: Aude Vauconsant
Cartography Update: Carte
Photography Credits: Alamy 4ML, 7, 42;
Diana Jarvis/Rough Guides 5M, 5MC, 6R,
7R, 12, 17, 19, 32, 35, 49, 91, 92, 100, 102,
104; Getty Images 5T, 5TC, 15, 21, 31, 38,
54, 61, 94; iStock 4MC, 4TL, 6L, 11, 29, 45,
57, 58, 62, 68, 71, 77, 79, 81, 83, 84; Nick
Miners/REX/Shutterstock 88; Shutterstock
1, 4TC, 5MC, 5M, 22, 26, 36, 46, 51, 52, 65,
66, 72, 75, 87, 96; Wolfgang Diederich/
imageBROKER/REX/Shutterstock 40
Cover Picture: Getty Images

Distribution
UK, Ireland and Europe: Apa Publications
(UK) Ltd; sales@insightguides.com
United States and Canada: Ingram
Publisher Services; ips@ingramcontent.com
Australia and New Zealand: Woodslane;
info@woodslane.com.au
Southeast Asia: Apa Publications (SN) Pte;
singaporeoffice@insightguides.com
Worldwide: Apa Publications (UK) Ltd;
sales@insightguides.com

**Special Sales, Content Licensing
and CoPublishing**
Insight Guides can be purchased in bulk
quantities at discounted prices. We can
create special editions, personalised jackets
and corporate imprints tailored to your
needs. sales@insightguides.com;
www.insightguides.biz

speaking your language

phrase book & dictionary
phrase book & CD

Available in: Arabic, Brazilian Portuguese*, Burmese*, Cantonese
Chinese, Croatian, Czech*, Danish*, Dutch, English, Filipino, Finnish*, French,
German, Greek, Hebrew*, Hindi*, Hungarian*, Indonesian, Italian, Japanese,
Korean, Latin American Spanish, Malay, Mandarin Chinese, Mexican Spanish,
Norwegian, Polish, Portuguese, Romanian*, Russian, Spanish, Swedish, Thai,
Turkish, Vietnamese
*Book only